I0329602

C-4095 CAREER EXAMINATION SERIES

This is your PASSBOOK for...

Call Center Representative

Test Preparation Study Guide
Questions & Answers

NLC®

NATIONAL LEARNING CORPORATION®

National Learning Corporation

212 Michael Drive, Syosset, NY 11791
(516) 921-8888 • www.passbooks.com
E-mail: info@passbooks.com

PUBLISHED IN THE UNITED STATES OF AMERICA

PASSBOOK® SERIES

THE *PASSBOOK® SERIES* has been created to prepare applicants and candidates for the ultimate academic battlefield – the examination room.

At some time in our lives, each and every one of us may be required to take an examination – for validation, matriculation, admission, qualification, registration, certification, or licensure.

Based on the assumption that every applicant or candidate has met the basic formal educational standards, has taken the required number of courses, and read the necessary texts, the *PASSBOOK® SERIES* furnishes the one special preparation which may assure passing with confidence, instead of failing with insecurity. Examination questions – together with answers – are furnished as the basic vehicle for study so that the mysteries of the examination and its compounding difficulties may be eliminated or diminished by a sure method.

This book is meant to help you pass your examination provided that you qualify and are serious in your objective.

The entire field is reviewed through the huge store of content information which is succinctly presented through a provocative and challenging approach – the question-and-answer method.

A climate of success is established by furnishing the correct answers at the end of each test.

You soon learn to recognize types of questions, forms of questions, and patterns of questioning. You may even begin to anticipate expected outcomes.

You perceive that many questions are repeated or adapted so that you can gain acute insights, which may enable you to score many sure points.

You learn how to confront new questions, or types of questions, and to attack them confidently and work out the correct answers.

You note objectives and emphases, and recognize pitfalls and dangers, so that you may make positive educational adjustments.

Moreover, you are kept fully informed in relation to new concepts, methods, practices, and directions in the field.

You discover that you are actually taking the examination all the time: you are preparing for the examination by "taking" an examination, not by reading extraneous and/or supererogatory textbooks.

In short, this PASSBOOK®, used directedly, should be an important factor in helping you to pass your test.

CALL CENTER REPRESENTATIVE

DUTIES

Under supervision, Call Center Representatives provide a single point of contact for all non-emergency city services utilizing state-of-the-art telephone and interactive computer systems; respond to phone inquiries from the public; provide customer service and information to callers; take complaints and service requests and forward them for further action; enter inquiries, complaints and requests into appropriate computer systems; and perform related clerical and computer work.

SCOPE OF THE EXAMINATION

The multiple-choice test may include questions on understanding written information; combining separate pieces of information to form a general conclusion; applying general rules to a specific situation; understanding the order in which things should be done; written communication (including spelling); ability to create accurate records of information exchanged with callers; and other related areas.

HOW TO TAKE A TEST

I. YOU MUST PASS AN EXAMINATION

A. WHAT EVERY CANDIDATE SHOULD KNOW

Examination applicants often ask us for help in preparing for the written test. What can I study in advance? What kinds of questions will be asked? How will the test be given? How will the papers be graded?

As an applicant for a civil service examination, you may be wondering about some of these things. Our purpose here is to suggest effective methods of advance study and to describe civil service examinations.

Your chances for success on this examination can be increased if you know how to prepare. Those "pre-examination jitters" can be reduced if you know what to expect. You can even experience an adventure in good citizenship if you know why civil service exams are given.

B. WHY ARE CIVIL SERVICE EXAMINATIONS GIVEN?

Civil service examinations are important to you in two ways. As a citizen, you want public jobs filled by employees who know how to do their work. As a job seeker, you want a fair chance to compete for that job on an equal footing with other candidates. The best-known means of accomplishing this two-fold goal is the competitive examination.

Exams are widely publicized throughout the nation. They may be administered for jobs in federal, state, city, municipal, town or village governments or agencies.

Any citizen may apply, with some limitations, such as the age or residence of applicants. Your experience and education may be reviewed to see whether you meet the requirements for the particular examination. When these requirements exist, they are reasonable and applied consistently to all applicants. Thus, a competitive examination may cause you some uneasiness now, but it is your privilege and safeguard.

C. HOW ARE CIVIL SERVICE EXAMS DEVELOPED?

Examinations are carefully written by trained technicians who are specialists in the field known as "psychological measurement," in consultation with recognized authorities in the field of work that the test will cover. These experts recommend the subject matter areas or skills to be tested; only those knowledges or skills important to your success on the job are included. The most reliable books and source materials available are used as references. Together, the experts and technicians judge the difficulty level of the questions.

Test technicians know how to phrase questions so that the problem is clearly stated. Their ethics do not permit "trick" or "catch" questions. Questions may have been tried out on sample groups, or subjected to statistical analysis, to determine their usefulness.

Written tests are often used in combination with performance tests, ratings of training and experience, and oral interviews. All of these measures combine to form the best-known means of finding the right person for the right job.

II. HOW TO PASS THE WRITTEN TEST

A. NATURE OF THE EXAMINATION

To prepare intelligently for civil service examinations, you should know how they differ from school examinations you have taken. In school you were assigned certain definite pages to read or subjects to cover. The examination questions were quite detailed and usually emphasized memory. Civil service exams, on the other hand, try to discover your present ability to perform the duties of a position, plus your potentiality to learn these duties. In other words, a civil service exam attempts to predict how successful you will be. Questions cover such a broad area that they cannot be as minute and detailed as school exam questions.

In the public service similar kinds of work, or positions, are grouped together in one "class." This process is known as *position-classification*. All the positions in a class are paid according to the salary range for that class. One class title covers all of these positions, and they are all tested by the same examination.

B. FOUR BASIC STEPS

1) Study the announcement

How, then, can you know what subjects to study? Our best answer is: "Learn as much as possible about the class of positions for which you've applied." The exam will test the knowledge, skills and abilities needed to do the work.

Your most valuable source of information about the position you want is the official exam announcement. This announcement lists the training and experience qualifications. Check these standards and apply only if you come reasonably close to meeting them.

The brief description of the position in the examination announcement offers some clues to the subjects which will be tested. Think about the job itself. Review the duties in your mind. Can you perform them, or are there some in which you are rusty? Fill in the blank spots in your preparation.

Many jurisdictions preview the written test in the exam announcement by including a section called "Knowledge and Abilities Required," "Scope of the Examination," or some similar heading. Here you will find out specifically what fields will be tested.

2) Review your own background

Once you learn in general what the position is all about, and what you need to know to do the work, ask yourself which subjects you already know fairly well and which need improvement. You may wonder whether to concentrate on improving your strong areas or on building some background in your fields of weakness. When the announcement has specified "some knowledge" or "considerable knowledge," or has used adjectives like "beginning principles of..." or "advanced ... methods," you can get a clue as to the number and difficulty of questions to be asked in any given field. More questions, and hence broader coverage, would be included for those subjects which are more important in the work. Now weigh your strengths and weaknesses against the job requirements and prepare accordingly.

3) Determine the level of the position

Another way to tell how intensively you should prepare is to understand the level of the job for which you are applying. Is it the entering level? In other words, is this the position in which beginners in a field of work are hired? Or is it an intermediate or advanced level? Sometimes this is indicated by such words as "Junior" or "Senior" in the class title. Other jurisdictions use Roman numerals to designate the level – Clerk I, Clerk II, for example. The word "Supervisor" sometimes appears in the title. If the level is not indicated by the title, check the description of duties. Will you be working under very close supervision, or will you have responsibility for independent decisions in this work?

4) Choose appropriate study materials

Now that you know the subjects to be examined and the relative amount of each subject to be covered, you can choose suitable study materials. For beginning level jobs, or even advanced ones, if you have a pronounced weakness in some aspect of your training, read a modern, standard textbook in that field. Be sure it is up to date and has general coverage. Such books are normally available at your library, and the librarian will be glad to help you locate one. For entry-level positions, questions of appropriate difficulty are chosen – neither highly advanced questions, nor those too simple. Such questions require careful thought but not advanced training.

If the position for which you are applying is technical or advanced, you will read more advanced, specialized material. If you are already familiar with the basic principles of your field, elementary textbooks would waste your time. Concentrate on advanced textbooks and technical periodicals. Think through the concepts and review difficult problems in your field.

These are all general sources. You can get more ideas on your own initiative, following these leads. For example, training manuals and publications of the government agency which employs workers in your field can be useful, particularly for technical and professional positions. A letter or visit to the government department involved may result in more specific study suggestions, and certainly will provide you with a more definite idea of the exact nature of the position you are seeking.

III. KINDS OF TESTS

Tests are used for purposes other than measuring knowledge and ability to perform specified duties. For some positions, it is equally important to test ability to make adjustments to new situations or to profit from training. In others, basic mental abilities not dependent on information are essential. Questions which test these things may not appear as pertinent to the duties of the position as those which test for knowledge and information. Yet they are often highly important parts of a fair examination. For very general questions, it is almost impossible to help you direct your study efforts. What we can do is to point out some of the more common of these general abilities needed in public service positions and describe some typical questions.

1) General information

Broad, general information has been found useful for predicting job success in some kinds of work. This is tested in a variety of ways, from vocabulary lists to questions about current events. Basic background in some field of work, such as sociology or economics, may be sampled in a group of questions. Often these are principles which have become familiar to most persons through exposure rather than through formal training. It is difficult to advise you how to study for these questions; being alert to the world around you is our best suggestion.

2) Verbal ability

An example of an ability needed in many positions is verbal or language ability. Verbal ability is, in brief, the ability to use and understand words. Vocabulary and grammar tests are typical measures of this ability. Reading comprehension or paragraph interpretation questions are common in many kinds of civil service tests. You are given a paragraph of written material and asked to find its central meaning.

3) Numerical ability

Number skills can be tested by the familiar arithmetic problem, by checking paired lists of numbers to see which are alike and which are different, or by interpreting charts and graphs. In the latter test, a graph may be printed in the test booklet which you are asked to use as the basis for answering questions.

4) Observation

A popular test for law-enforcement positions is the observation test. A picture is shown to you for several minutes, then taken away. Questions about the picture test your ability to observe both details and larger elements.

5) Following directions

In many positions in the public service, the employee must be able to carry out written instructions dependably and accurately. You may be given a chart with several columns, each column listing a variety of information. The questions require you to carry out directions involving the information given in the chart.

6) Skills and aptitudes

Performance tests effectively measure some manual skills and aptitudes. When the skill is one in which you are trained, such as typing or shorthand, you can practice. These tests are often very much like those given in business school or high school courses. For many of the other skills and aptitudes, however, no short-time preparation can be made. Skills and abilities natural to you or that you have developed throughout your lifetime are being tested.

Many of the general questions just described provide all the data needed to answer the questions and ask you to use your reasoning ability to find the answers. Your best preparation for these tests, as well as for tests of facts and ideas, is to be at your physical and mental best. You, no doubt, have your own methods of getting into an exam-taking mood and keeping "in shape." The next section lists some ideas on this subject.

IV. KINDS OF QUESTIONS

Only rarely is the "essay" question, which you answer in narrative form, used in civil service tests. Civil service tests are usually of the short-answer type. Full instructions for answering these questions will be given to you at the examination. But in case this is your first experience with short-answer questions and separate answer sheets, here is what you need to know:

1) Multiple-choice Questions

Most popular of the short-answer questions is the "multiple choice" or "best answer" question. It can be used, for example, to test for factual knowledge, ability to solve problems or judgment in meeting situations found at work.

A multiple-choice question is normally one of three types—

- It can begin with an incomplete statement followed by several possible endings. You are to find the one ending which *best* completes the statement, although some of the others may not be entirely wrong.
- It can also be a complete statement in the form of a question which is answered by choosing one of the statements listed.

- It can be in the form of a problem – again you select the best answer.

Here is an example of a multiple-choice question with a discussion which should give you some clues as to the method for choosing the right answer:

When an employee has a complaint about his assignment, the action which will *best* help him overcome his difficulty is to

A. discuss his difficulty with his coworkers
B. take the problem to the head of the organization
C. take the problem to the person who gave him the assignment
D. say nothing to anyone about his complaint

In answering this question, you should study each of the choices to find which is best. Consider choice "A" – Certainly an employee may discuss his complaint with fellow employees, but no change or improvement can result, and the complaint remains unresolved. Choice "B" is a poor choice since the head of the organization probably does not know what assignment you have been given, and taking your problem to him is known as "going over the head" of the supervisor. The supervisor, or person who made the assignment, is the person who can clarify it or correct any injustice. Choice "C" is, therefore, correct. To say nothing, as in choice "D," is unwise. Supervisors have and interest in knowing the problems employees are facing, and the employee is seeking a solution to his problem.

2) True/False Questions

The "true/false" or "right/wrong" form of question is sometimes used. Here a complete statement is given. Your job is to decide whether the statement is right or wrong.

SAMPLE: A roaming cell-phone call to a nearby city costs less than a non-roaming call to a distant city.

This statement is wrong, or false, since roaming calls are more expensive.

This is not a complete list of all possible question forms, although most of the others are variations of these common types. You will always get complete directions for answering questions. Be sure you understand *how* to mark your answers – ask questions until you do.

V. RECORDING YOUR ANSWERS

Computer terminals are used more and more today for many different kinds of exams.

For an examination with very few applicants, you may be told to record your answers in the test booklet itself. Separate answer sheets are much more common. If this separate answer sheet is to be scored by machine – and this is often the case – it is highly important that you mark your answers correctly in order to get credit.

An electronic scoring machine is often used in civil service offices because of the speed with which papers can be scored. Machine-scored answer sheets must be marked with a pencil, which will be given to you. This pencil has a high graphite content which responds to the electronic scoring machine. As a matter of fact, stray dots may register as answers, so do not let your pencil rest on the answer sheet while you are pondering the correct answer. Also, if your pencil lead breaks or is otherwise defective, ask for another.

Since the answer sheet will be dropped in a slot in the scoring machine, be careful not to bend the corners or get the paper crumpled.

The answer sheet normally has five vertical columns of numbers, with 30 numbers to a column. These numbers correspond to the question numbers in your test booklet. After each number, going across the page are four or five pairs of dotted lines. These short dotted lines have small letters or numbers above them. The first two pairs may also have a "T" or "F" above the letters. This indicates that the first two pairs only are to be used if the questions are of the true-false type. If the questions are multiple choice, disregard the "T" and "F" and pay attention only to the small letters or numbers.

Answer your questions in the manner of the sample that follows:

32. The largest city in the United States is
    - A. Washington, D.C.
    - B. New York City
    - C. Chicago
    - D. Detroit
    - E. San Francisco

1) Choose the answer you think is best. (New York City is the largest, so "B" is correct.)
2) Find the row of dotted lines numbered the same as the question you are answering. (Find row number 32)
3) Find the pair of dotted lines corresponding to the answer. (Find the pair of lines under the mark "B.")
4) Make a solid black mark between the dotted lines.

VI. BEFORE THE TEST

Common sense will help you find procedures to follow to get ready for an examination. Too many of us, however, overlook these sensible measures. Indeed, nervousness and fatigue have been found to be the most serious reasons why applicants fail to do their best on civil service tests. Here is a list of reminders:

- Begin your preparation early – Don't wait until the last minute to go scurrying around for books and materials or to find out what the position is all about.
- Prepare continuously – An hour a night for a week is better than an all-night cram session. This has been definitely established. What is more, a night a week for a month will return better dividends than crowding your study into a shorter period of time.
- Locate the place of the exam – You have been sent a notice telling you when and where to report for the examination. If the location is in a different town or otherwise unfamiliar to you, it would be well to inquire the best route and learn something about the building.
- Relax the night before the test – Allow your mind to rest. Do not study at all that night. Plan some mild recreation or diversion; then go to bed early and get a good night's sleep.
- Get up early enough to make a leisurely trip to the place for the test – This way unforeseen events, traffic snarls, unfamiliar buildings, etc. will not upset you.
- Dress comfortably – A written test is not a fashion show. You will be known by number and not by name, so wear something comfortable.

- Leave excess paraphernalia at home – Shopping bags and odd bundles will get in your way. You need bring only the items mentioned in the official notice you received; usually everything you need is provided. Do not bring reference books to the exam. They will only confuse those last minutes and be taken away from you when in the test room.
- Arrive somewhat ahead of time – If because of transportation schedules you must get there very early, bring a newspaper or magazine to take your mind off yourself while waiting.
- Locate the examination room – When you have found the proper room, you will be directed to the seat or part of the room where you will sit. Sometimes you are given a sheet of instructions to read while you are waiting. Do not fill out any forms until you are told to do so; just read them and be prepared.
- Relax and prepare to listen to the instructions
- If you have any physical problem that may keep you from doing your best, be sure to tell the test administrator. If you are sick or in poor health, you really cannot do your best on the exam. You can come back and take the test some other time.

VII. AT THE TEST

The day of the test is here and you have the test booklet in your hand. The temptation to get going is very strong. Caution! There is more to success than knowing the right answers. You must know how to identify your papers and understand variations in the type of short-answer question used in this particular examination. Follow these suggestions for maximum results from your efforts:

1) Cooperate with the monitor

The test administrator has a duty to create a situation in which you can be as much at ease as possible. He will give instructions, tell you when to begin, check to see that you are marking your answer sheet correctly, and so on. He is not there to guard you, although he will see that your competitors do not take unfair advantage. He wants to help you do your best.

2) Listen to all instructions

Don't jump the gun! Wait until you understand all directions. In most civil service tests you get more time than you need to answer the questions. So don't be in a hurry. Read each word of instructions until you clearly understand the meaning. Study the examples, listen to all announcements and follow directions. Ask questions if you do not understand what to do.

3) Identify your papers

Civil service exams are usually identified by number only. You will be assigned a number; you must not put your name on your test papers. Be sure to copy your number correctly. Since more than one exam may be given, copy your exact examination title.

4) Plan your time

Unless you are told that a test is a "speed" or "rate of work" test, speed itself is usually not important. Time enough to answer all the questions will be provided, but this does not mean that you have all day. An overall time limit has been set. Divide the total time (in minutes) by the number of questions to determine the approximate time you have for each question.

5) Do not linger over difficult questions

If you come across a difficult question, mark it with a paper clip (useful to have along) and come back to it when you have been through the booklet. One caution if you do this – be sure to skip a number on your answer sheet as well. Check often to be sure that you have not lost your place and that you are marking in the row numbered the same as the question you are answering.

6) Read the questions

Be sure you know what the question asks! Many capable people are unsuccessful because they failed to *read* the questions correctly.

7) Answer all questions

Unless you have been instructed that a penalty will be deducted for incorrect answers, it is better to guess than to omit a question.

8) Speed tests

It is often better NOT to guess on speed tests. It has been found that on timed tests people are tempted to spend the last few seconds before time is called in marking answers at random – without even reading them – in the hope of picking up a few extra points. To discourage this practice, the instructions may warn you that your score will be "corrected" for guessing. That is, a penalty will be applied. The incorrect answers will be deducted from the correct ones, or some other penalty formula will be used.

9) Review your answers

If you finish before time is called, go back to the questions you guessed or omitted to give them further thought. Review other answers if you have time.

10) Return your test materials

If you are ready to leave before others have finished or time is called, take ALL your materials to the monitor and leave quietly. Never take any test material with you. The monitor can discover whose papers are not complete, and taking a test booklet may be grounds for disqualification.

VIII. EXAMINATION TECHNIQUES

1) Read the general instructions carefully. These are usually printed on the first page of the exam booklet. As a rule, these instructions refer to the timing of the examination; the fact that you should not start work until the signal and must stop work at a signal, etc. If there are any *special* instructions, such as a choice of questions to be answered, make sure that you note this instruction carefully.

2) When you are ready to start work on the examination, that is as soon as the signal has been given, read the instructions to each question booklet, underline any key words or phrases, such as *least*, *best*, *outline*, *describe* and the like. In this way you will tend to answer as requested rather than discover on reviewing your paper that you *listed without describing*, that you selected the *worst* choice rather than the *best* choice, etc.

3) If the examination is of the objective or multiple-choice type – that is, each question will also give a series of possible answers: A, B, C or D, and you are called upon to select the best answer and write the letter next to that answer on your answer paper – it is advisable to start answering each question in turn. There may be anywhere from 50 to 100 such questions in the three or four hours allotted and you can see how much time would be taken if you read through all the questions before beginning to answer any. Furthermore, if you come across a question or group of questions which you know would be difficult to answer, it would undoubtedly affect your handling of all the other questions.

4) If the examination is of the essay type and contains but a few questions, it is a moot point as to whether you should read all the questions before starting to answer any one. Of course, if you are given a choice – say five out of seven and the like – then it is essential to read all the questions so you can eliminate the two that are most difficult. If, however, you are asked to answer all the questions, there may be danger in trying to answer the easiest one first because you may find that you will spend too much time on it. The best technique is to answer the first question, then proceed to the second, etc.

5) Time your answers. Before the exam begins, write down the time it started, then add the time allowed for the examination and write down the time it must be completed, then divide the time available somewhat as follows:
   - If 3-1/2 hours are allowed, that would be 210 minutes. If you have 80 objective-type questions, that would be an average of 2-1/2 minutes per question. Allow yourself no more than 2 minutes per question, or a total of 160 minutes, which will permit about 50 minutes to review.
   - If for the time allotment of 210 minutes there are 7 essay questions to answer, that would average about 30 minutes a question. Give yourself only 25 minutes per question so that you have about 35 minutes to review.

6) The most important instruction is to *read each question* and make sure you know what is wanted. The second most important instruction is to *time yourself properly* so that you answer every question. The third most important instruction is to *answer every question*. Guess if you have to but include something for each question. Remember that you will receive no credit for a blank and will probably receive some credit if you write something in answer to an essay question. If you guess a letter – say "B" for a multiple-choice question – you may have guessed right. If you leave a blank as an answer to a multiple-choice question, the examiners may respect your feelings but it will not add a point to your score. Some exams may penalize you for wrong answers, so in such cases *only*, you may not want to guess unless you have some basis for your answer.

7) Suggestions
   a. Objective-type questions
      1. Examine the question booklet for proper sequence of pages and questions
      2. Read all instructions carefully
      3. Skip any question which seems too difficult; return to it after all other questions have been answered
      4. Apportion your time properly; do not spend too much time on any single question or group of questions

5. Note and underline key words – *all, most, fewest, least, best, worst, same, opposite,* etc.
6. Pay particular attention to negatives
7. Note unusual option, e.g., unduly long, short, complex, different or similar in content to the body of the question
8. Observe the use of "hedging" words – *probably, may, most likely,* etc.
9. Make sure that your answer is put next to the same number as the question
10. Do not second-guess unless you have good reason to believe the second answer is definitely more correct
11. Cross out original answer if you decide another answer is more accurate; do not erase until you are ready to hand your paper in
12. Answer all questions; guess unless instructed otherwise
13. Leave time for review

b. Essay questions
1. Read each question carefully
2. Determine exactly what is wanted. Underline key words or phrases.
3. Decide on outline or paragraph answer
4. Include many different points and elements unless asked to develop any one or two points or elements
5. Show impartiality by giving pros and cons unless directed to select one side only
6. Make and write down any assumptions you find necessary to answer the questions
7. Watch your English, grammar, punctuation and choice of words
8. Time your answers; don't crowd material

8) Answering the essay question

Most essay questions can be answered by framing the specific response around several key words or ideas. Here are a few such key words or ideas:

M's: manpower, materials, methods, money, management
P's: purpose, program, policy, plan, procedure, practice, problems, pitfalls, personnel, public relations

a. Six basic steps in handling problems:
1. Preliminary plan and background development
2. Collect information, data and facts
3. Analyze and interpret information, data and facts
4. Analyze and develop solutions as well as make recommendations
5. Prepare report and sell recommendations
6. Install recommendations and follow up effectiveness

b. Pitfalls to avoid
1. *Taking things for granted* – A statement of the situation does not necessarily imply that each of the elements is necessarily true; for example, a complaint may be invalid and biased so that all that can be taken for granted is that a complaint has been registered

2. *Considering only one side of a situation* – Wherever possible, indicate several alternatives and then point out the reasons you selected the best one
3. *Failing to indicate follow up* – Whenever your answer indicates action on your part, make certain that you will take proper follow-up action to see how successful your recommendations, procedures or actions turn out to be
4. *Taking too long in answering any single question* – Remember to time your answers properly

IX. AFTER THE TEST

Scoring procedures differ in detail among civil service jurisdictions although the general principles are the same. Whether the papers are hand-scored or graded by machine we have described, they are nearly always graded by number. That is, the person who marks the paper knows only the number – never the name – of the applicant. Not until all the papers have been graded will they be matched with names. If other tests, such as training and experience or oral interview ratings have been given, scores will be combined. Different parts of the examination usually have different weights. For example, the written test might count 60 percent of the final grade, and a rating of training and experience 40 percent. In many jurisdictions, veterans will have a certain number of points added to their grades.

After the final grade has been determined, the names are placed in grade order and an eligible list is established. There are various methods for resolving ties between those who get the same final grade – probably the most common is to place first the name of the person whose application was received first. Job offers are made from the eligible list in the order the names appear on it. You will be notified of your grade and your rank as soon as all these computations have been made. This will be done as rapidly as possible.

People who are found to meet the requirements in the announcement are called "eligibles." Their names are put on a list of eligible candidates. An eligible's chances of getting a job depend on how high he stands on this list and how fast agencies are filling jobs from the list.

When a job is to be filled from a list of eligibles, the agency asks for the names of people on the list of eligibles for that job. When the civil service commission receives this request, it sends to the agency the names of the three people highest on this list. Or, if the job to be filled has specialized requirements, the office sends the agency the names of the top three persons who meet these requirements from the general list.

The appointing officer makes a choice from among the three people whose names were sent to him. If the selected person accepts the appointment, the names of the others are put back on the list to be considered for future openings.

That is the rule in hiring from all kinds of eligible lists, whether they are for typist, carpenter, chemist, or something else. For every vacancy, the appointing officer has his choice of any one of the top three eligibles on the list. This explains why the person whose name is on top of the list sometimes does not get an appointment when some of the persons lower on the list do. If the appointing officer chooses the second or third eligible, the No. 1 eligible does not get a job at once, but stays on the list until he is appointed or the list is terminated.

X. HOW TO PASS THE INTERVIEW TEST

The examination for which you applied requires an oral interview test. You have already taken the written test and you are now being called for the interview test – the final part of the formal examination.

You may think that it is not possible to prepare for an interview test and that there are no procedures to follow during an interview. Our purpose is to point out some things you can do in advance that will help you and some good rules to follow and pitfalls to avoid while you are being interviewed.

What is an interview supposed to test?

The written examination is designed to test the technical knowledge and competence of the candidate; the oral is designed to evaluate intangible qualities, not readily measured otherwise, and to establish a list showing the relative fitness of each candidate – as measured against his competitors – for the position sought. Scoring is not on the basis of "right" and "wrong," but on a sliding scale of values ranging from "not passable" to "outstanding." As a matter of fact, it is possible to achieve a relatively low score without a single "incorrect" answer because of evident weakness in the qualities being measured.

Occasionally, an examination may consist entirely of an oral test – either an individual or a group oral. In such cases, information is sought concerning the technical knowledges and abilities of the candidate, since there has been no written examination for this purpose. More commonly, however, an oral test is used to supplement a written examination.

Who conducts interviews?

The composition of oral boards varies among different jurisdictions. In nearly all, a representative of the personnel department serves as chairman. One of the members of the board may be a representative of the department in which the candidate would work. In some cases, "outside experts" are used, and, frequently, a businessman or some other representative of the general public is asked to serve. Labor and management or other special groups may be represented. The aim is to secure the services of experts in the appropriate field.

However the board is composed, it is a good idea (and not at all improper or unethical) to ascertain in advance of the interview who the members are and what groups they represent. When you are introduced to them, you will have some idea of their backgrounds and interests, and at least you will not stutter and stammer over their names.

What should be done before the interview?

While knowledge about the board members is useful and takes some of the surprise element out of the interview, there is other preparation which is more substantive. It *is* possible to prepare for an oral interview – in several ways:

1) Keep a copy of your application and review it carefully before the interview

This may be the only document before the oral board, and the starting point of the interview. Know what education and experience you have listed there, and the sequence and dates of all of it. Sometimes the board will ask you to review the highlights of your experience for them; you should not have to hem and haw doing it.

2) Study the class specification and the examination announcement

Usually, the oral board has one or both of these to guide them. The qualities, characteristics or knowledges required by the position sought are stated in these documents. They offer valuable clues as to the nature of the oral interview. For example, if the job involves supervisory responsibilities, the announcement will usually indicate that knowledge of modern supervisory methods and the qualifications of the candidate as a supervisor will be tested. If so, you can expect such questions, frequently in the form of a hypothetical situation which you are expected to solve. NEVER go into an oral without knowledge of the duties and responsibilities of the job you seek.

3) Think through each qualification required

Try to visualize the kind of questions you would ask if you were a board member. How well could you answer them? Try especially to appraise your own knowledge and background in each area, *measured against the job sought*, and identify any areas in which you are weak. Be critical and realistic – do not flatter yourself.

4) Do some general reading in areas in which you feel you may be weak

For example, if the job involves supervision and your past experience has NOT, some general reading in supervisory methods and practices, particularly in the field of human relations, might be useful. Do NOT study agency procedures or detailed manuals. The oral board will be testing your understanding and capacity, not your memory.

5) Get a good night's sleep and watch your general health and mental attitude

You will want a clear head at the interview. Take care of a cold or any other minor ailment, and of course, no hangovers.

What should be done on the day of the interview?

Now comes the day of the interview itself. Give yourself plenty of time to get there. Plan to arrive somewhat ahead of the scheduled time, particularly if your appointment is in the fore part of the day. If a previous candidate fails to appear, the board might be ready for you a bit early. By early afternoon an oral board is almost invariably behind schedule if there are many candidates, and you may have to wait. Take along a book or magazine to read, or your application to review, but leave any extraneous material in the waiting room when you go in for your interview. In any event, relax and compose yourself.

The matter of dress is important. The board is forming impressions about you – from your experience, your manners, your attitude, and your appearance. Give your personal appearance careful attention. Dress your best, but not your flashiest. Choose conservative, appropriate clothing, and be sure it is immaculate. This is a business interview, and your appearance should indicate that you regard it as such. Besides, being well groomed and properly dressed will help boost your confidence.

Sooner or later, someone will call your name and escort you into the interview room. *This is it.* From here on you are on your own. It is too late for any more preparation. But remember, you asked for this opportunity to prove your fitness, and you are here because your request was granted.

What happens when you go in?

The usual sequence of events will be as follows: The clerk (who is often the board stenographer) will introduce you to the chairman of the oral board, who will introduce you to the other members of the board. Acknowledge the introductions before you sit down. Do not be surprised if you find a microphone facing you or a stenotypist sitting by. Oral interviews are usually recorded in the event of an appeal or other review.

Usually the chairman of the board will open the interview by reviewing the highlights of your education and work experience from your application – primarily for the benefit of the other members of the board, as well as to get the material into the record. Do not interrupt or comment unless there is an error or significant misinterpretation; if that is the case, do not hesitate. But do not quibble about insignificant matters. Also, he will usually ask you some question about your education, experience or your present job – partly to get you to start talking and to establish the interviewing "rapport." He may start the actual questioning, or turn it over to one of the other members. Frequently, each member undertakes the questioning on a particular area, one in which he is perhaps most competent, so you can expect each member to participate in the examination. Because time is limited, you may also expect some rather abrupt switches in the direction the questioning takes, so do not be upset by it. Normally, a board member will not pursue a single line of questioning unless he discovers a particular strength or weakness.

After each member has participated, the chairman will usually ask whether any member has any further questions, then will ask you if you have anything you wish to add. Unless you are expecting this question, it may floor you. Worse, it may start you off on an extended, extemporaneous speech. The board is not usually seeking more information. The question is principally to offer you a last opportunity to present further qualifications or to indicate that you have nothing to add. So, if you feel that a significant qualification or characteristic has been overlooked, it is proper to point it out in a sentence or so. Do not compliment the board on the thoroughness of their examination – they have been sketchy, and you know it. If you wish, merely say, "No thank you, I have nothing further to add." This is a point where you can "talk yourself out" of a good impression or fail to present an important bit of information. Remember, *you close the interview yourself.*

The chairman will then say, "That is all, Mr. _______, thank you." Do not be startled; the interview is over, and quicker than you think. Thank him, gather your belongings and take your leave. Save your sigh of relief for the other side of the door.

How to put your best foot forward

Throughout this entire process, you may feel that the board individually and collectively is trying to pierce your defenses, seek out your hidden weaknesses and embarrass and confuse you. Actually, this is not true. They are obliged to make an appraisal of your qualifications for the job you are seeking, and they want to see you in your best light. Remember, they must interview all candidates and a non-cooperative candidate may become a failure in spite of their best efforts to bring out his qualifications. Here are 15 suggestions that will help you:

1) Be natural – Keep your attitude confident, not cocky

If you are not confident that you can do the job, do not expect the board to be. Do not apologize for your weaknesses, try to bring out your strong points. The board is interested in a positive, not negative, presentation. Cockiness will antagonize any board member and make him wonder if you are covering up a weakness by a false show of strength.

2) Get comfortable, but don't lounge or sprawl

Sit erectly but not stiffly. A careless posture may lead the board to conclude that you are careless in other things, or at least that you are not impressed by the importance of the occasion. Either conclusion is natural, even if incorrect. Do not fuss with your clothing, a pencil or an ashtray. Your hands may occasionally be useful to emphasize a point; do not let them become a point of distraction.

3) Do not wisecrack or make small talk

This is a serious situation, and your attitude should show that you consider it as such. Further, the time of the board is limited – they do not want to waste it, and neither should you.

4) Do not exaggerate your experience or abilities

In the first place, from information in the application or other interviews and sources, the board may know more about you than you think. Secondly, you probably will not get away with it. An experienced board is rather adept at spotting such a situation, so do not take the chance.

5) If you know a board member, do not make a point of it, yet do not hide it

Certainly you are not fooling him, and probably not the other members of the board. Do not try to take advantage of your acquaintanceship – it will probably do you little good.

6) Do not dominate the interview

Let the board do that. They will give you the clues – do not assume that you have to do all the talking. Realize that the board has a number of questions to ask you, and do not try to take up all the interview time by showing off your extensive knowledge of the answer to the first one.

7) Be attentive

You only have 20 minutes or so, and you should keep your attention at its sharpest throughout. When a member is addressing a problem or question to you, give him your undivided attention. Address your reply principally to him, but do not exclude the other board members.

8) Do not interrupt

A board member may be stating a problem for you to analyze. He will ask you a question when the time comes. Let him state the problem, and wait for the question.

9) Make sure you understand the question

Do not try to answer until you are sure what the question is. If it is not clear, restate it in your own words or ask the board member to clarify it for you. However, do not haggle about minor elements.

10) Reply promptly but not hastily

A common entry on oral board rating sheets is "candidate responded readily," or "candidate hesitated in replies." Respond as promptly and quickly as you can, but do not jump to a hasty, ill-considered answer.

11) Do not be peremptory in your answers

A brief answer is proper – but do not fire your answer back. That is a losing game from your point of view. The board member can probably ask questions much faster than you can answer them.

12) Do not try to create the answer you think the board member wants

He is interested in what kind of mind you have and how it works – not in playing games. Furthermore, he can usually spot this practice and will actually grade you down on it.

13) Do not switch sides in your reply merely to agree with a board member

Frequently, a member will take a contrary position merely to draw you out and to see if you are willing and able to defend your point of view. Do not start a debate, yet do not surrender a good position. If a position is worth taking, it is worth defending.

14) Do not be afraid to admit an error in judgment if you are shown to be wrong

The board knows that you are forced to reply without any opportunity for careful consideration. Your answer may be demonstrably wrong. If so, admit it and get on with the interview.

15) Do not dwell at length on your present job

The opening question may relate to your present assignment. Answer the question but do not go into an extended discussion. You are being examined for a *new* job, not your present one. As a matter of fact, try to phrase ALL your answers in terms of the job for which you are being examined.

Basis of Rating

Probably you will forget most of these "do's" and "don'ts" when you walk into the oral interview room. Even remembering them all will not ensure you a passing grade. Perhaps you did not have the qualifications in the first place. But remembering them will help you to put your best foot forward, without treading on the toes of the board members.

Rumor and popular opinion to the contrary notwithstanding, an oral board wants you to make the best appearance possible. They know you are under pressure – but they also want to see how you respond to it as a guide to what your reaction would be under the pressures of the job you seek. They will be influenced by the degree of poise you display, the personal traits you show and the manner in which you respond.

ABOUT THIS BOOK

This book contains tests divided into Examination Sections. Go through each test, answering every question in the margin. We have also attached a sample answer sheet at the back of the book that can be removed and used. At the end of each test look at the answer key and check your answers. On the ones you got wrong, look at the right answer choice and learn. Do not fill in the answers first. Do not memorize the questions and answers, but understand the answer and principles involved. On your test, the questions will likely be different from the samples. Questions are changed and new ones added. If you understand these past questions you should have success with any changes that arise. Tests may consist of several types of questions. We have additional books on each subject should more study be advisable or necessary for you. Finally, the more you study, the better prepared you will be. This book is intended to be the last thing you study before you walk into the examination room. Prior study of relevant texts is also recommended. NLC publishes some of these in our Fundamental Series. Knowledge and good sense are important factors in passing your exam. Good luck also helps. So now study this Passbook, absorb the material contained within and take that knowledge into the examination. Then do your best to pass that exam.

EXAMINATION SECTION

EXAMINATION SECTION

TEST 1

DIRECTIONS: Each question or incomplete statement is followed by several suggested answers or completions. Select the one that BEST answers the question or completes the statement. *PRINT THE LETTER OF THE CORRECT ANSWER IN THE SPACE AT THE RIGHT.*

1. You answer a phone complaint from a person concerning an improper labeling practice in a shop in his neighborhood. Upon listening to the complaint, you get the impression that the person is exaggerating and may be too excited to view the matter clearly. 1.____
Of the following, your BEST course would be to
   A. tell the man that you can understand his anger but think it is not a really serious problem
   B. suggest to the man that he file a complaint with the Department of Consumer Affairs
   C. tell the man to stay away from the shop and have his friends do the same
   D. take down the information that the man offers so that he will see that the Police Department is concerned

2. Suppose that late at night you receive a call on 911. The caller turns out to be an elderly man who is not able to get out much and who is calling you not because he needs help but because he wants to talk with someone. 2.____
The BEST way to handle such a situation is to
   A. explain to him that the number is for emergencies and his call may prevent others from getting the help they need
   B. talk to him if not many calls are coming in but excuse yourself and cut him off if you are busy
   C. cut him off immediately when you find out he does not need help because this will be the most effective way of discouraging him
   D. suggest that he call train or bus information as the clerks there are often not busy at night

3. While you are on duty, you receive a call from a person whose name your recognize to be that of a person who calls frequently about matters of no importance. The caller requests your name and your supervisor's name so that she can report you for being impolite to her. 3.____
You should
   A. ask her when and how you were impolite to her
   B. tell her that she should not call about such minor matters
   C. make a report about her complaint for your superior
   D. give her the information that she requests

4. Of the following, the MOST important reason for requiring each employ of the Police Department to be responsible for good public relations is that 4.____
   A. the Police Department has better morale when employees join in an effort to improve public relations
   B. the public judges the Department according to impressions received at every level in the Department
   C. most employees will not behave well toward the public unless required to do so
   D. employees who improve public relations will receive commendations from superiors

5. Assume that you are in the Bureau of Public Relations. You receive a telephone call from a citizen who asks if a study has been made of the advisability of combining the city's police and fire departments. Assume that you have no information on the subject. 5.____
   Of the following, your BEST course would be to
   A. tell the caller that undoubtedly the subject has been studied but that you do not have the information available
   B. suggest to the caller that he telephone the Fire Department's Community Relations section for further information
   C. explain to the caller that the functions of the two departments are distinct and that combining them would be inefficient
   D. take the caller's number in order to call back, and then find information or referrals to give him

6. Suppose that Police Department officials have discouraged representatives of the press from contacting police administrative aides (except aides in the Public Relations Bureau) for information. 6.____
   Of the following, the BEST reason for such a policy would be to
   A. assure proper control over information released to the press by the Department
   B. increase the value of official press releases of the Department
   C. make press representatives realize that the Department is not seeking publicity
   D. reduce the chance of crimes being committed in imitation of those reported in the press

7. People who phone the Police Department often use excited, emotional, and sometimes angry speech. 7.____
   The BEST policy for you to take when speaking to this type of caller is to
   A. tell the person directly that he must speak in a more civil way
   B. tell the caller to call back when he is in a better mood
   C. give the person time to settle down, by doing most of the talking yourself
   D. speak calmly yourself to help the caller to gradually become more relaxed

8. On a particularly busy evening, the police administrative aide assigned to the telephones had answered a tremendous number of inquiries and complaints by irate citizens. His patience was exhausted when he received a call from a citizen who reported, *Officer, a bird just flew into my bedroom. What should I do?* In a release of tension, the aide responded, *Keep it for seven days; and if no one claims it, it is yours.* 8.____
This response by the aide would usually be considered
   A. *advisable*, because the person should see how unusual his question was
   B. *advisable*, because he avoided offering police services that were unavailable
   C. *not advisable*, because such a remark might be regarded as insulting rather than humorous
   D. *not advisable*, because the person might not want a bird for a pet

9. While temporarily assigned to switchboard duty, you receive a call from a man who says his uncle in Pittsburgh has just called him and threatened to commit suicide. The man is convinced his uncle intends to carry out his threat. 9.____
Of the following, you should
   A. advise the man to have neighbors of the uncle check to see if the uncle is all right
   B. politely inform the man that such out-of-town incidents are beyond the authority of the local precinct
   C. take the uncle's name, address, and telephone number and immediately contact police authorities in Pittsburgh
   D. get the man's name, address, and telephone number so that you can determine whether the call is a hoax

10. Assume that in the course of your assigned duties you have just taken a necessary action which you feel has angered a citizen. After he has gone, you suddenly realize that the incident might result in an unjustified complaint. 10.____
The MOST advisable action for you to take now would be to
   A. contact the person and apologize to him
   B. make complete notes on the incident and on any witnesses who might be helpful
   C. ask your superior what you might expect in case of such a complaint, without giving any hint of the actual occurrence
   D. accept the situation as one of the hazards of your job

11. Your job may bring you in contact with people from the community who are confronted with emergencies,, and are experiencing feelings of tension, anxiety, or even hostility. It is good to keep in mind what attitude is most helpful to people who, in such situations like these. 11.____
Which of the following would be BEST to do?
   A. Present similar examples of your own problems to make the person feel that his problems are not unusual.
   B. Recognize the person's feelings, present information on available services, and make suggestions as to proper procedures

C. Expect that some of the information is exaggerated and encourage the person to let some time pass before seeking further help.
D. Have the person wait while you try to make arrangements for his problem to be solved.

12. Suppose that while on duty you receive a call from the owner of a gas station which is located within the precinct. The owner is annoyed with a certain rule made by the Police Department which concerns the operation of such stations. You agree with him. 12.____
Of the following, the BEST action for you to take is to
A. make a report on the call and suggest to the owner that he write a letter to the Department about the rule
B. tell the owner that there is little that can be done since such rules are departmental policy
C. tell the owner that you agree with his complaint and that you will write a memo of his call
D. establish good relations with the owner by suggesting how to word a letter that will get action from the department

13. Suppose that you are working at the switchboard when a call comes in late at night from a woman who reports that her neighbors are having a very noisy party. She gives you her first name, surname, and address, and you ask her title is *Miss* or *Mrs.* She replies that her title is irrelevant to her complaint, and wants to know why you ask. 13.____
Of the following possible ways of handling this, which is BEST?
A. Insist that the title is necessary for identification purposes
B. Tell her that it is merely to find out what her marital status is
C. Agree that the information is not necessary and ask her how she wants to be referred to
D. Find out why she shows such a peculiar reaction to a request for harmless information

14. While covering an assignment on the switchboard, you receive a call from a young girl who tells you of rumored plans for a gang fight in her neighborhood. You should 14.____
A. take down the information so that a patrol squad can investigate the area and possibly keep the fight from starting
B. discourage the girl from becoming alarmed by reminding her that it is only a rumor
C. realize that this is a teenager looking for attention, humor her, and dismiss the matter
D. take down the information but tell the girl that you need concrete information, and not just rumors, to take any action on her call

15. The one of the following which would MOST likely lead to friction among police administrative aides in a unit would be for the supervisor in charge of the unit to 15.____
A. defend the actions of the aides he supervises when discussing them with his own supervisor

B. get his men to work together as a team in completing the work of the unit
C. praise each of the aides he supervises *in confidence* as the best aide in the unit
D. consider the point of view of the aides he supervises when assigning unpleasant tasks

16. Suppose that a police administrative aide who had been transferred to your office from another unit in your Department because of difficulties with his supervisor has been placed under your supervision. 16.____
The BEST course of action for you to take FIRST is to
A. analyze the aide's past grievance to determine if the transfer was the best settlement of the problem
B. advise him of the difficulties his former supervisor had with other employees and encourage him not to feel bad about the transfer
C. warn him that you will not tolerate any nonsense and that he will be watched carefully while assigned to your unit
D. instruct him in the duties he will be performing in your unit and make him feel *wanted* in his new position

17. In which of the following circumstances would it be MOST appropriate for you to use an impersonal style of writing rather than a personal style, which relies on the use of personal pronouns and other personal references? 17.____
When writing a memorandum to
A. give your opinion to an associate on the advisability of holding a weekly staff meeting
B. furnish your superior with data justifying a proposed outlay of funds for new equipment
C. give your version of an incident which resulted in a complaint by a citizen about your behavior
D. support your request for a transfer to another division

18. A newly appointed supervisor should learn as much as possible about the backgrounds of his subordinates. 18.____
The statement is generally CORRECT because
A. effective handling of subordinates is based upon knowledge of their individual differences
B. knowing their backgrounds assures they will be treated objectively, equally, and without favor
C. some subordinates perform more efficiently under one supervisor than under another
D subordinates have confidence in a supervisor who knows all about them

19. You have found it necessary, for valid reasons, to criticize the work of one of the female police administrative aides. She later comes to your desk and accuses you of criticizing her work because she is a woman. 19.____
The BEST way for you to deal with this employee is to
A. ask her to apologize, since you would never allow yourself to be guilty of his kind of discrimination

B. discuss her complaint with her, explaining again and at greater length the reason for your criticism
C. assure her you wish to be fair, and ask her to submit a written report to you on her complaint
D. apologize for hurting her feelings and promise that she will be left alone in the future

20. The following steps are recognized steps in teaching an employee a new skill: 20.____
I. Demonstrate how to do the work
II. Let the learner do the work himself
III. Explain the nature and purpose of the work
IV. Correct poor procedures by suggestion and demonstration
The CORRECT order for these steps is
A. III, II, IV, I B. II, I, III, IV C. III, I, II, IV D. I, III, II, IV

21. Suppose you have arranged an interview with a subordinate to try to help him overcome a serious shortcoming in his technical work. While you do not intend to talk to him about his attitude, you have noticed that he seems to be suspicious and resentful of people in authority. You need a record of the points covered in the discussion since further interviews are likely to be necessary. 21.____
Your BEST course would be to
A. write a checklist of points you wish to discuss and carefully check the points off as the interview progresses
B. know exactly how you wish to proceed, and then make written notes during the interview of your subordinate's comments
C. frankly tell your subordinate that you are recording the talk on tape but place the recorder where it will not hinder discussion
D. keep in mind what you wish to accomplish and make notes on the interview immediately after it is over

22. A police administrative aide has explained a complicated procedure to several subordinates. He has been talking clearly, allowing time for information to sink in. He has also encouraged questions. Yet, he still questions his subordinates after his explanation, with the obvious objective of finding out whether they completely understand the procedure. 22.____
Under these circumstances, the action of the police administrative aide, in asking questions about the procedure, is
A. *not advisable*, because subordinates who do not now know the procedure which has been explained so carefully can read and study it
B. *not advisable*, because he endangers his relationship with his subordinates by insulting their intelligence
C. *advisable*, because subordinate basically resent instructions and seldom give their full attention in a group situation
D. *advisable*, because the answers to his questions help him to determine whether he has gained his objective

23. The most competent of the police administrative aides is a pleasant, intelligent young woman who breaks the rules of the Department by occasionally making long personal telephone calls during working hours. You have not talked to her up until now about this fault. However, the calls are beginning to increase, and you decide to deal directly with the problem. 23.____
The BEST way to approach the subject with her would be to
   A. review with her the history of her infractions of the rules
   B. point out that her conduct is not fair to the other workers
   C. tell her that her personal calls are excessive and discuss it with her
   D. warn her quietly that you intend to apply penalties if necessary

24. Assume that you are supervising eight male police administrative aides who do similar clerical work. A group of four of them work on each side of a row of files which can be moved without much trouble. You notice that in each group there is a clique of three aides, leaving one member isolated. The two isolated members are relative newcomers. 24.____
Your BEST course in such a case would be to
   A. ignore the situation because to concern yourself with informal social arrangements of your subordinates would distract you from more important matters
   B. ask each of the cliques to invite the isolated member in their working group to lunch with them from time to time
   C. tell each group that you cannot allow cliques to form as it is bad for the morale of the unit
   D. find an excuse to move the file cabinet to the side of the room and then move the desks of the two isolated members close together

25. Suppose that your supervisor, who has recently been promoted and transferred to your division, asks you to review a certain procedure with a view to its possible revision. You know that several years ago a sergeant made a lengthy and intensive report based on a similar review. 25.____
Which of the following would it be BEST for you to do FIRST?
   A. Ask your supervisor if he is aware of the previous report
   B. Read the sergeant's report before you begin work to see what bearing it has on your assignment
   C. Begin work on the review without reading his report so that you will have a fresh point of view
   D. Ask the sergeant to assist you in your review

26. Using form letters in business correspondence is LEAST effective when 26.____
   A. answering letters on a frequently recurring subject
   B. giving the same information to many addresses
   C. the recipient is only interested in the routing information contained in the form letter
   D. a reply must be keyed to the individual requirements of the intended reader

27. From the viewpoint of an office administrator, the BEST of the following reasons for distributing the incoming mail before the beginning of the regular work day is that 27.____
   A. distribution can be handled quickly and most efficiently at that time
   B. distribution later in the day may be distracting to or interfering with other employees
   C. the employees who distribute the mail can then perform other tasks during the rest of the day
   D. office activities for the day based on the mail may then be started promptly

28. Suppose you have had difficulty locating a document in the files because you could not decide where it should have been filed. You learn that other people in the office have had the same problem. You know that the document will be needed from time to time in the future. 28.____
Your BEST course, when refiling the document, would be to
   A. make a written note of where you found it so that you will find it more easily the next time
   B. reclassify it and file it in the file where you first looked for it
   C. file it where you found it and put cross-reference sheets in the other likely files
   D. make a mental association to help you find it the next time and put it back where you found it

29. Suppose that your supervisor is attending a series of meetings of police captains in Philadelphia and will not be back until next Wednesday. He has left no instructions with you as to how you should handle telephone calls for him. 29.____
In most instances, your BEST course of action would be to say:
   A. He isn't here just now.
   B. He is out of town and won't be back until next Wednesday.
   C. He won't be in today.
   D. He is in Philadelphia attending a meeting of police captains.

30. The one of the following which is USUALLY an important by-product of the preparation of a procedure manual is that 30.____
   A. information uncovered in the process of preparation may lead to improvement of procedures
   B. workers refer to the manual instead of bothering their supervisors for information
   C. supervisors use the manual for training stenographers
   D. employees have equal access to information needed to do their jobs

31. You have been asked to organize a clerical job and supervise police administrative aides who will do the actual work. The job consists of removing, from several boxes of data processing cards which are arranged in alphabetical order, the cards of those whose names appear on certain lists. The person removing the card then notes a date on the card. Assume that the work will be done accurately whatever system is used. 31.____

Which of the following statements describes both the MOST efficient method and the BEST reasons for using that method? Have

A. two aides work together, one calling names and the other extracting cards, and dating them, because the average production of any two aides working together should be higher, under these circumstances, than that of any two aides working alone
B. each aide work alone, because it is easier to check spelling when reading the names than when listening to them
C. two aides work together, one calling names and the other extracting cards and dating them, because social interaction tends to make work go faster
D. each aide work alone, because the average production of any two aides, each working alone, should be higher, under these circumstances, than that of any two aides working together

32. The term *work flow*, when used in connection with office management or the activities in an office GENERALLY means the 32.____

A. rate of speed at which work flows through a single section of an office
B. use of charts in the analysis of various office functions
C. number of individual work units which can be produced by the average employee
D. step-by-step physical routing of work through its various procedures

Questions 33-40.

DIRECTIONS:

Name of Offense	V	A	N	D	S	B	R	U	G	H
Code Letter	c	o	m	p	l	e	x	i	t	y
File Number	1	2	3	4	5	6	7	8	9	0

Assume that each of the above capital letters is the first letter of the name of an offense, that the small letter directly beneath each capita letter is the code letter for the offense, and that the number directly beneath each code letter is the file number for the offense.

In each of Questions 33 through 40, the code letters and file numbers should correspond to the capital letters.

If there is an error only in Column 2, mark your answer A.

If there is an error only in Column 3, mark your answer B.

If there is an error in both Column 2 and Column, mark your answer C.

If both Columns 2 and 3 are correct, mark your answer D.

Sample Questions:

COLUMN 1	COLUMN 2	COLUMN 3
BNARGHSVVU	emoxtylcci	6357905118

The code letters in Column 2 are correct, but the first 5 in Column 3 should be 2. Therefore, the answer is B.

	COLUMN 1	COLUMN 2	COLUMN 3	
33.	HGDSBNBSVR	ytplxmelcx	0945736517	33._____

34.	SDGUUNHVAH	lptiimycoy	5498830120	34.____
35.	BRSNAAVUDU	exlmooctpi	6753221848	35.____
36.	VSRUDNADUS	cleipmopil	1568432485	36.____
37.	NDSHVRBUAG	mplycxeiot	3450175829	37.____
38.	GHUSNVBRDA	tyilmcexpo	9805316742	38.____
39.	DBSHVURANG	pesycixomt	4650187239	39.____
40.	RHNNASBDGU	xymnolepti	7033256398	40.____

KEY (CORRECT ANSWERS)

1.	B	11.	B	21.	D	31.	D
2.	A	12.	A	22.	D	32.	D
3.	D	13.	C	23.	C	33.	C
4.	B	14.	A	24.	D	34.	D
5.	D	15.	C	25.	A	35.	A
6.	A	16.	D	26.	D	36.	C
7.	D	17.	B	27.	D	37.	B
8.	C	18.	A	28.	C	38.	D
9.	C	19.	B	29.	B	39.	A
10.	B	20.	C	30.	A	40.	C

EXAMINATION SECTION

TEST 1

DIRECTIONS: Each question or incomplete statement is followed by several suggested answers or completions. Select the one that BEST answers the question or completes the statement. *PRINT THE LETTER OF THE CORRECT ANSWER IN THE SPACE AT THE RIGHT.*

Questions 1-8.

DIRECTIONS: Each of Questions 1 through 8 consists of a statement which contains a word (one of those underlined) that is either incorrectly used because it is not in keeping with the meaning the quotation is evidently intended to convey or is misspelled. There is only one INCORRECT word in each quotation. Of the four underlined words, determine if the first one should be replaced by the word lettered A, the second replaced by the word lettered B, the third replaced by the word lettered C, or the fourth replaced by the word lettered D. Print the letter of the replacement word you have selected in the space at the right.

1. Whether one depends on fluorescent or artificial light or both, adequate standards should be maintained by means of systematic tests. 1.____
   A. natural B. safeguards C. established D. routine

2. An officer has to be prepared to assume his knowledge as a social scientist in the community. 2.____
   A. forced B. role C. philosopher D. street

3. It is practically impossible to indicate whether a sentence is too long simply by measuring its length. 3.____
   A. almost B. tell C. very D. guessing

4. Strong leaders are required to organize a community for delinquency prevention and for dissemination of organized crime and drug addiction. 4.____
   A. tactics B. important C. control D. meetings

5. The demonstrators, who were taken to the Criminal Courts building in Manhattan (because it was large enough to accommodate them), contended that the arrests were unwarrented. 5.____
   A. exhibitors B. legions C. adjudicate D. unwarranted

6. The were guaranteed a calm atmosphere, free from harassment, which would be conducive to quiet consideration of the indictments. 6.____
   A. guaranteed B. atmospher C. harassment D. inditements

7. The alleged killer was occasionally permitted to excercise in the corridor. 7.____
   A. alledged B. ocasionally C. permited D. exercise

8. Defense <u>counsel</u> stated, in <u>affect</u>, that <u>their</u> conduct was <u>permissable</u> under the First Amendment. 8.____
   A. council B. effect C. there D. permissable

Questions 9-12.

DIRECTIONS: Each of the two sentences in Questions 9 through 12 may be correct or may contain errors in punctuation, capitalization, or grammar. If there is an error only in sentence I, mark your answer A. If there is an error in both sentence I and sentence II, mark your answer C. If both sentence I and sentence II are correct, mark your answer D.

9. I. It is very annoying to have a pencil sharpener, which is not in working order. 9.____
   II. Officer Blake checked the door of Joe's Restaurant and found that the lock has been jammed.

10. I. When you are studying a good textbook is important. 10.____
    II. He said he would divide the money equally between you and me.

11. I. Since he went on the city council a year ago, one of his primary concerns has been safety in the streets. 11.____
    II. After waiting in the doorway for about 15 minutes, a black sedan appeared.

12. I. The question is, "What is the difference between a lawful and an unlawful demonstration?" 12.____
    II. The captain assigned two detectives, John and I, to the investigation.

Questions 13-14.

DIRECTIONS: In each of Questions 13 and 14, the four sentences are from a paragraph in a report. They are not in the right order. Which of the following arrangement is the BEST one?

13. I. Most organizations favor one of the types but always include the others to a lesser degree. 13.____
    II. However, we can detect a definite trend toward greater use of symbolic control.
    III. We suggest that our local police agencies are today primarily utilizing material control.
    IV. Control can be classified into three types: physical, material, and symbolic.
    The CORRECT answer is:
    A. IV, II III, I B. II, I, IV, III C. III, IV, II, I D. IV, I, III, II

14. I They can and do take advantage of ancient political and geographical boundaries, which often give them sanctuary from effective policy activity. 14.____
    II. This country is essentially a country of small police forces, each operating independently within the limits of its jurisdiction.

III. The boundaries that define and limit police operations do not hinder the movement of criminals, of course.
IV. The machinery of law enforcement in America is fragmented, complicated, and frequently overlapping.
The CORRECT answer is
A. III, I, II, IV B. II, IV, I, III C. IV, II, III, I D. IV, III, II, I

15. Generally, the frequency with which reports are to be submitted or the length of the interval which they cover should depend MAINLY on the 15.____
A. amount of time needed to prepare the reports
B. degree of comprehensiveness required in the reports
C. availability of the data to be included in the reports
D. extent of the variations in the data with the passage of time

16. Suppose you have to write a report on a serious infraction of rules by one of the police administrative aides you supervise. The circumstances in which the infraction occurred are quite complicated. 16.____
The BEST way to organize this report would be to
A. give all points equal emphasis throughout the report
B. include more than one point in a paragraph only if necessary to equalize the size of paragraphs
C. place the least important points before the most important points
D. present each significant point in a separate paragraph

17. Suppose that police expenses in the city in a certain year amounted to 7.5% of total expenses. 17.____
In indicating this percentage on a *pie* or circular chart, which is 360, the size of the angle between the two radiuses would be MOST NEARLY
A. 3.7 B. 7.5 C. 27 D. 54

18. Suppose that in police precinct A, where there are 4,180 children, 627 children entered a contest sponsored by the Police Community Relations Bureau. In precinct B, where there were 7,840 children, 1,960 children entered the contest. 18.____
The total percentage of all children in both precincts who entered the contest amounted to MOST NEARLY
A. 19.5% B. 20% C. 21.5% D. 22.5%

19. If Circle A represents Police Administrative Aides (PAA's) who scored above 85 on a PAA test and Circle B represents PAA's who scored above 85 on a Senior PAA test, then the diagram at the right means that 19.____

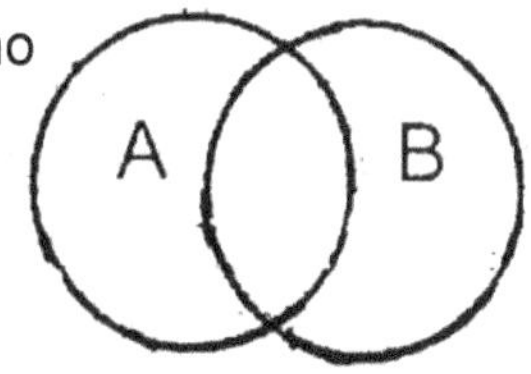

A. no PAA who scored above 85 on a PAA test scored above 85 on the Senior PAA test
B. the majority of PAA's who scored above 85 on a PAA test scored above 85 on the Senior PAA test
C. there were some PAA's who did not take the Senior PAA test
D. some PAA's who scored above 85 on a PAA test scored above 85 on the Senior PAA test

20. Suppose that in 1912 the city had a population of 550,000 and a police force of 200, and that in 2012 the city had a population of 8,000,000 and a police force of 32,000. 20.____
If the ratio of police to population in 2012 is compared with the same ratio in 1912, what is the resulting relationship of the 2012 ratio to the 1912 ratio?
A. 160:11 B. 160:1 C. 16:1 D. 11:1

Questions 21-24.

DIRECTIONS: Questions 21 through 24 are to be answered SOLELY on the basis of the information contained in the following passage.

Of those arrested in the city in 2019 for felonies or misdemeanors, only 32% were found guilty of any charge. Fifty-six percent of such arrestees were acquitted or had their cases dismissed, 11% failed to appear for trial, and 1% received other dispositions. Of those found guilty, only 7.4% received any sentences of over one year in jail. Only 50% of those found guilty were sentenced to any further time in jail. When considered with the low probability of arrests for most crimes, these figures make it clear that the crime control system in the city poses little threat to the average criminal. Delay compounds the problem. The average case took four appearances for disposition after arraignment. Twenty percent of all cases took eight or more appearances to reach a disposition. Forty-four percent of all cases took more than one year to disposition.

21. According to the above passage, crime statistics for 2019 indicate that 21.____
A. there is a low probability of arrests for all crimes in the city
B. the average criminal has much to fear from the law in the city
C. over 10% of arrestees in the city charged with felonies or misdemeanors did not show up for trial
D. criminals in the city are less likely to be caught than criminals in the rest f the country

22. The percentage of those arrested in 2019 who received sentences of over one year in jail amounted MOST NEARLY to 22.____
A. .237 B. 2.4 C. 23.7 D. 24.0

23. According to the above passage, the percentage of arrestees in 2019 who were found guilty was 23.____
A 20% of those arrested for misdemeanors
B. 11% of those arrested for felonies
C. 50% of those sentenced to further time in jail
D. 32% of those arrested for felonies or misdemeanors

24. According to the above passage, the number of appearances after arraignment and before disposition amounted to 24.____
A. an average of four
B. eight or more in 44% of the cases
C. over four for cases which took more than a year
D. between four and eight for most cases

Questions 25-27.

DIRECTIONS: Questions 25 through 27 are to be answered SOLELY on the basis of the information contained in the following passage.

The traditional characteristics of a police organization, which do not foster group-centered leadership, are being changed daily by progressive police administrators. These characteristics are authoritarian and result in a leader-centered style with all determination of policy and procedure made by the leader. In the group-centered style, policies and procedures are a matter for group discussion and decision. The supposedly modern view is that the group-centered style is the most conducive to improving organizational effectiveness. By contrast, the traditional view regards the group-centered style as an idealistic notion of psychologists. It is questionable, however, that the situation determines the appropriate leadership style. In some circumstances, it will be leader-centered; in others, group-centered. Nevertheless, police supervisors will see more situations calling for a leadership style that, while flexible, is primarily group-centered. Thus, the supervisor in a police department must have a capacity not just to issue orders but to engage in behavior involving organizational leadership which primarily emphasizes goals and work facilitation.

25. According to the above passage, there is reason to believe that with regard to the effectiveness of different types of leadership, the — 25.____
    A. leader-centered type is better than the individual-centered type or the group-centered type
    B. leader-centered type is best in some situations and the group-centered type best in other situations
    C. group-centered type is better than the leader-centered type in all situations
    D. authoritarian type is least effective in democratic countries

26. According to the above passage, police administrators today are — 26.____
    A. more likely than in the past to favor making decisions on the basis of discussions with subordinates
    B. likely in general to favor traditional patterns of leadership in their organizations
    C. more likely to be progressive than conservative
    D. practical and individualistic rather than idealistic in their approach to police problems

27. According to the above passage, the role of the police department is changing in such a way that its supervisors must — 27.____
    A. give greater consideration to the needs of individual subordinates
    B. be more flexible in dealing with infractions of department rules
    C. provide leadership which stresses the goals of the department and helps the staff to reach them
    D. refrain from issuing orders and allow subordinates to decide how to carry out their assignments

Questions 28-31.

DIRECTIONS: Questions 28 through 31 are to be answered SOLELY on the basis of the information contained in the following passage.

Under the provisions of the Bank Protection Act of 1968, enacted July 8, 1968, each Federal banking supervisory agency, as of January 7, 1969, had to issue rules establishing minimum standards with which financial institutions under their control must comply with respect to the installation, maintenance, and operation of security devices and procedures, reasonable in cost, to discourage robberies, burglaries, and larcenies, and to assist in the identification and apprehension of persons who commit such acts. The rules set the time limits within which the affected banks and savings and loan associations must comply with the standards, and the rules require the submission of periodic reports on the steps taken. A violator of a rule under this Act is subject to a civil penalty not to exceed $100 for each day of the violation. The enforcement of these regulations rests with the responsible banking supervisory agencies.

28. The Bank Protection Act of 1968 was designed to 28.____
    A. provide Federal police protection for banks covered by the Act
    B. have organizations covered by the Act take precautions against criminals
    C. set up a system for reporting all bank robberies to the FBI
    D. insure institutions covered by the Act from financial loss due to robberies, burglaries, and larcenies

29. Under the provisions of the Bank Protection Act of 1968, each Federal banking supervisory agency was required to set up rules for financial institutions covered by the Act governing the 29.____
    A. hiring of personnel
    B. punishment of burglars
    C. taking of protective measures
    D. penalties for violations

30. Financial institutions covered by the Bank Protection Act of 1968 were required to 30.____
    A. file reports at regular intervals on what they had done to prevent theft
    B. identify and apprehend persons who commit robberies, burglaries, and larcenies
    C. draw up a code of ethics for their employees
    D. have fingerprints of their employees filed with the FBI

31. Under the provisions of the Bank Protection Act of 1968, a bank which is subject to the rules established under the Act and which violates a rule is liable to a penalty of NOT _____ than $100 for each _____. 31.____
    A. more; violation
    B. less; day of violation
    C. less; violation
    D. more; day of violation

Questions 32-36.

DIRECTIONS: Questions 32 through 36 are to be answered SOLELY on the basis of the information contained in the following passage.

A statement which is offered in an attempt to prove the truth of the matters therein stated, but which is not made by the author as a witness before the court at the particular trial in which it is so offered, is hearsay. This is so whether the statement consists of words (oral or written), of symbols used as a substitute for words, or of signs or other conduct offered as the equivalent of a statement. Subject to some well-established exceptions, hearsay is not generally acceptable as evidence, and it does not become competent evidence just because it is received by the court without objection. One basis for this rule is simply that a fact cannot be proved by showing that somebody stated it was a fact. Another basis for the rule is the fundamental principle that in a criminal prosecution the testimony of the witness shall be taken before the court, so that at the time he gives the testimony offered in evidence he will be sworn and subject to cross-examination, the scrutiny of the court, and confrontation by the accused.

32. Which of the following is hearsay? A(n) 32.____
   A. written statement by a person not present at the court hearing where the statement is submitted as proof of an occurrence
   B. oral statement in court by a witness of what he saw
   C. written statement of what he saw by a witness present in court
   D. re-enactment by a witness in court of what he saw

33. In a criminal case, a statement by a person not present in court is 33.____
   A. *acceptable* evidence if not objected to by the prosecutor
   B. *acceptable* evidence if not objected to by the defense lawyer
   C. *not acceptable* evidence except in certain well-settled circumstances
   D. *not acceptable* evidence under any circumstances

34. The rule on hearsay is founded on the belief that 34.____
   A. proving someone said an act occurred is not proof that the act did occur
   B. a person who has knowledge about a case should be willing to appear in court
   C. persons not present in court are likely to be unreliable witnesses
   D. permitting persons to testify without appearing in court will lead to a disrespect for law

35. One reason for the general rule that a witness in a criminal case must give his testimony in court is that 35.____
   A. a witness may be influenced by threats to make untrue statements
   B. the opposite side is then permitted to question him
   C. the court provides protection for a witness against unfair questioning
   D. the adversary system is designed to prevent a miscarriage of justice

36. Of the following, the MOST appropriate title for the above passage would be 36.____
   A. What is Hearsay
   B. Rights of Defendants
   C. Trial procedures
   D. Testimony of Witnesses

Questions 37-40.

DIRECTIONS: Questions 37 through 40 are to be answered SOLELY on the basis of the following graphs.

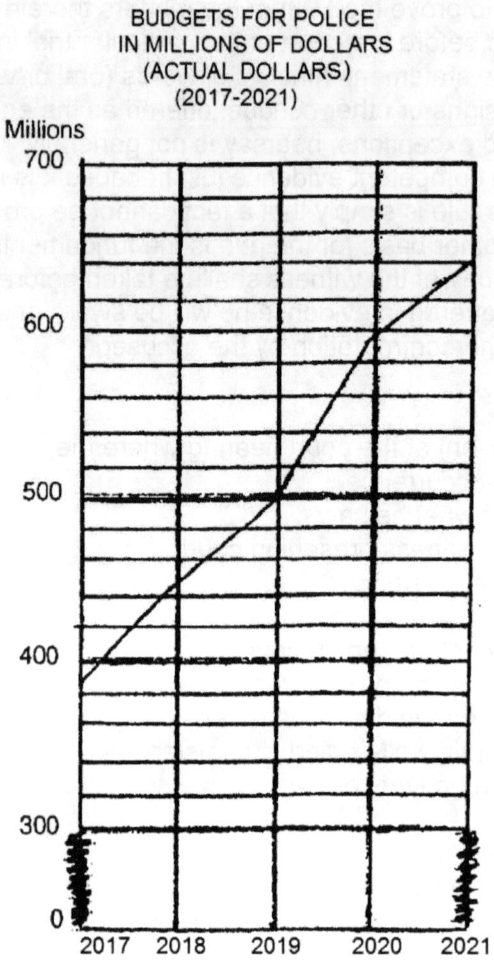

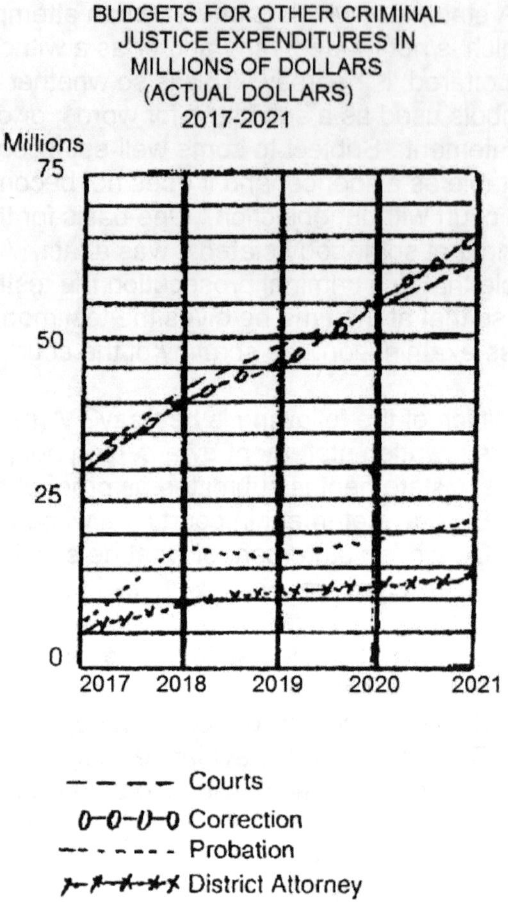

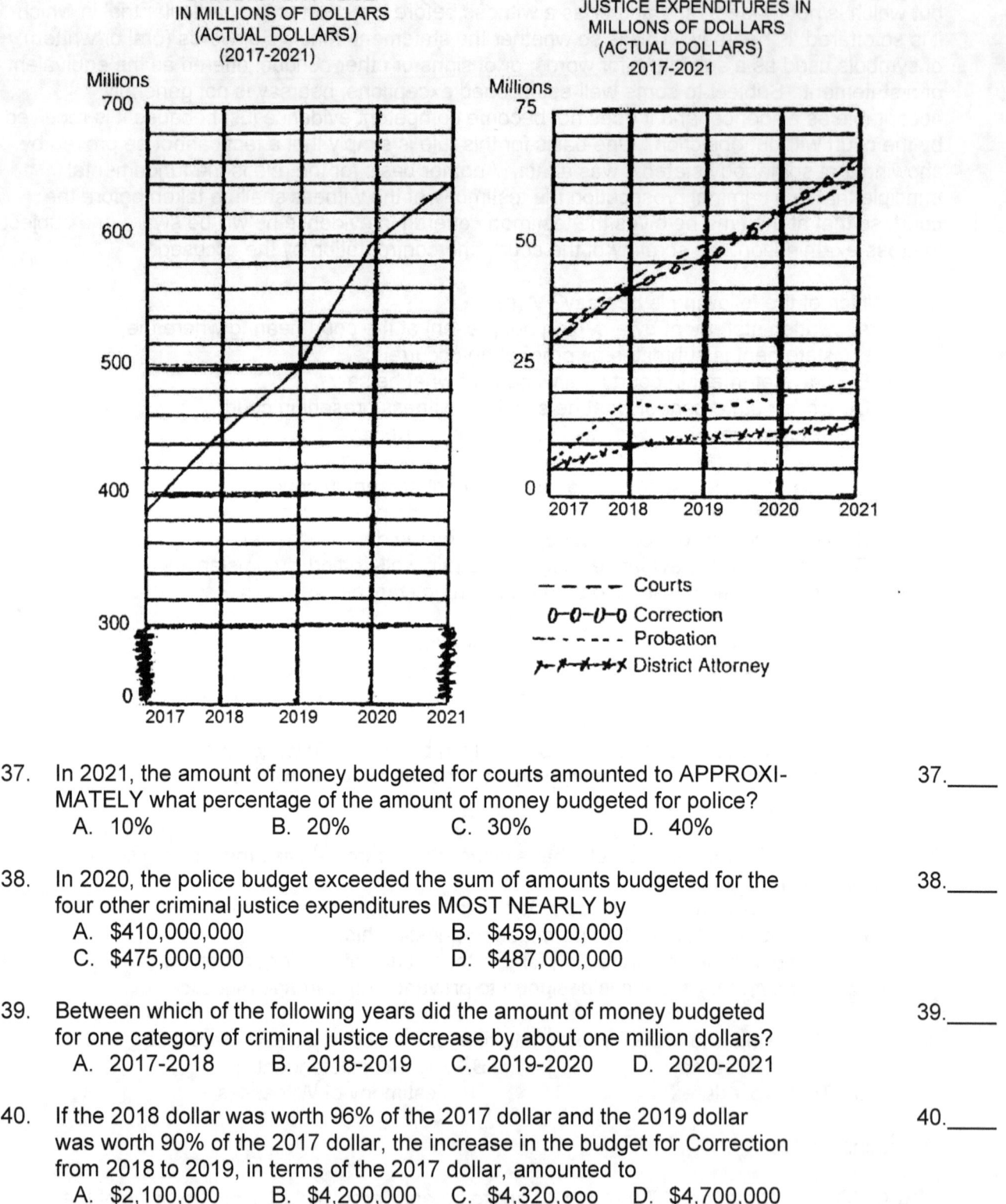

37. In 2021, the amount of money budgeted for courts amounted to APPROXIMATELY what percentage of the amount of money budgeted for police? 37.____
   A. 10% B. 20% C. 30% D. 40%

38. In 2020, the police budget exceeded the sum of amounts budgeted for the four other criminal justice expenditures MOST NEARLY by 38.____
   A. $410,000,000 B. $459,000,000
   C. $475,000,000 D. $487,000,000

39. Between which of the following years did the amount of money budgeted for one category of criminal justice decrease by about one million dollars? 39.____
   A. 2017-2018 B. 2018-2019 C. 2019-2020 D. 2020-2021

40. If the 2018 dollar was worth 96% of the 2017 dollar and the 2019 dollar was worth 90% of the 2017 dollar, the increase in the budget for Correction from 2018 to 2019, in terms of the 2017 dollar, amounted to 40.____
   A. $2,100,000 B. $4,200,000 C. $4,320,ooo D. $4,700,000

KEY (CORRECT ANSWERS)

1.	A	11.	C	21.	C	31.	D
2.	B	12.	B	22.	B	32.	A
3.	B	13.	D	23.	D	33.	C
4.	C	14.	C	24.	A	34.	A
5.	D	15.	D	25.	B	35.	B
6.	C	16.	D	26.	A	36.	A
7.	D	17.	C	27.	C	37.	A
8.	B	18.	C	28.	B	38.	B
9.	C	19.	D	29.	C	39.	B
10.	A	20.	D	30.	A	40.	A

EXAMINATION SECTION

TEST 1

DIRECTIONS: Each question or incomplete statement is followed by several suggested answers or completions. Select the one that BEST answers the question or completes the statement. *PRINT THE LETTER OF THE CORRECT ANSWER IN THE SPACE AT THE RIGHT.*

1. You are operating the switchboard and you receive an outside call for an extension line which is busy. 1.____
The one of the following which you should do FIRST is to
   A. ask the caller to try again later
   B. ask the caller to wait and inform him every thirty seconds about the status of the extension line
   C. tell the caller the line is busy and ask him if he wishes to wait
   D. tell the caller the line is busy and that you will connect him as soon as possible

2. A person comes to your work area. He makes comments which make no sense, gives foolish opinions, and tells you that he has enemies who are after him. He appears to be mentally ill. 2.____
Of the following, the FIRST action to take is to
   A. humor him by agreeing and sympathize with him
   B. try to reason with him and point out that his fears or opinions are unfounded
   C. have him arrested immediately
   D. tell him to leave at once

3. You are speaking with someone on the telephone who asks you a question which you cannot answer. You estimate that you can probably obtain the requested information in about five minutes. 3.____
Of the following, the MOST appropriate course of action would be to tell the caller that
   A. the information will take a short while to obtain, and then ask her for her name and number so that you can call her back when you have the information
   B. the information is available now, but she should call back later
   C. you do not know the answer and refer her to another division you think might be of service
   D. she is being placed on *hold* and that you will be with her in about five minutes

4. A person with a very heavy foreign accent comes to your work area and starts talking to you. He is very excited and is speaking too rapidly for you to understand what he is saying. 4.____
Of the following, the FIRST action for you to take is to

A. refer the person to your supervisor
B. continue your work and ignore the person in the hope that he will be discouraged and leave the building
C. ask or motion to the person to speak more slowly and have him repeat what he is trying to communicate
D. assume that the person is making a complaint, tell him that his problem will be taken care of, and then go back to your work

5. Assume that you are responsible for handling supplies. You notice that you are running low on a particular type of manila file folder exceptionally fast. You believe that someone in the precinct is taking the folders for other than official use. 5.____
In this situation, the one of the following that you should do FIRST is to
A. put up a notice stating that supplies have been disappearing and ask for the staff's cooperation in eliminating the problem
B. speak to your supervisor about the matter and let him decide on a course of action
C. watch the supply cabinet to determine who is taking the folders
D. ignore the situation and put in a requisition for additional folders

6. One afternoon, several of the officers ask you to perform different tasks. Each task requires a half day of work. Each officer tells you that his assignment must be finished by 4 P.M. the next day. 6.____
Of the following, the BEST way to handle this situation is to
A. do the assignments as quickly as you can, in the order in which the officers handed them to you
B. do some work on each assignment in the order of the ranks of the assigning officers and hand in as much as you are able to finish
C. speak to your immediate supervisor in order to determine the priority of assignments
D. accept all four assignments but explain to the last officer that you may not be able to finish his job

7. Every morning, several officers congregate around your work station during their breaks. You find their conversations very distracting. 7.____
The one of the following which you should do FIRST is to
A. ask them to cooperate with you by taking their breaks somewhere else
B. concentrate as best you can because their breaks do not last very long
C. reschedule your break to coincide with theirs
D. tell your supervisor that the officers are very uncooperative

8. One evening when you are very busy, you answer the phone and find that you are speaking with one of the neighborhood cranks, an elderly man who constantly complains that his neighbors are noisy. 8.____
In this situation, the MOST appropriate action for you to take is to
A. hang up and go on with your work
B. note the complaint and process it in the usual way
C. tell the man that his complaint will be investigated and then forget about it
D. tell the man that you are very buy and ask him to call back later

9. One morning you answer a telephone call for Lieutenant Jones, who is busy on another line. You inform the caller that Lieutenant Jones is on another line and this party says he will hold. After two minutes, Lieutenant Jones is still speaking on the first call. 9.____
Of the following, the FIRST thing for you to do is to
   A. ask the second caller whether it is an emergency
   B. signal Lieutenant Jones to let him know there is another call waiting for him
   C. request that the second caller try again later
   D. inform the second caller that Lieutenant Jones' line is still busy

10. The files in your office have been overcrowded and difficult to work with since you started working there. One day your supervisor is transferred and another aide in your office decides to discard three drawers of the oldest materials. 10.____
For him to take this action is
   A. *desirable*; it will facilitate handling the more active materials
   B. *undesirable*; no file should be removed from its point of origin
   C. *desirable*; there is no need to burden a new supervisor with unnecessary information
   D. *undesirable*; no file should be discarded without first noting what material has been discarded

11. You have been criticized by the lieutenant-in-charge because of spelling errors in some of your typing. You have only copied the reports as written, and you realize that the errors occurred in work given to you by Sergeant X. 11.____
Of the following, the BEST way for you to handle this situation is to
   A. tell the lieutenant that the spelling errors are Sergeant X's, not yours, because they occur only when you type his reports
   B. tell the lieutenant that you only type the reports as given to you, without implicating anyone
   C. inform Sergeant X that you have been unjustly criticized because of his spelling errors and politely request that he be more careful in the future
   D. use a dictionary whenever you have doubt regarding spelling

12. You have recently found several items misfiled. You believe that this occurred because a new administrative aide in your section has been making mistakes. 12.____
The BEST course of action for you to take is to
   A. refile the material and say nothing about it
   B. send your supervisor an anonymous note of complaint about the filing errors
   C. show the errors to the new administrative aide and tell him why they are errors in filing
   D. tell your supervisor that the new administrative aide makes a lot of errors in filing

13. One of your duties is to record information on a standard printed form regarding missing cars. One call you receive concerns a custom-built auto which has apparently been stolen. There seems to be no place on the form for many of the details which the owner gives you. 13.____

Of the following, the BEST way for you to obtain an adequate description of this car would be to

A. complete the form as best you can and attach another sheet containing the additional information the owner gives you
B. complete the form as best you can and request that the owner submit a photograph of the missing car
C. scrap the form since it is inadequate in this case and make out a report based on the information the owner gives you
D. complete the form as best you can and ignore extraneous information that the form does not call for

14. One weekend, you develop a painful infection in one hand. You know that your typing speed will be much slower than normal, and the likelihood of your making mistakes will be increased. 14.____
Of the following, the BEST course of action for you to take in this situation is to

A. report to work as scheduled and do your typing assignments as best you can without complaining
B. report to work as scheduled and ask your co-workers to divide your typing assignments until your hand heals
C. report to work as scheduled and ask your supervisor for non-typing assignments until your hand heals
D. call in sick and remain on medical leave until your hand is completely healed so that you can perform your normal duties

15. When filling out a departmental form during an interview concerning a citizen complaint, an administrative aide should know the purpose of each question that he asks the citizen. 15.____
For such information to be supplied by the department is

A. *advisable*, because the aide may lose interest in the job if he is not fully informed about the questions he has to ask
B. *inadvisable*, because the aide may reveal the true purpose of the questions to the citizens
C. *advisable*, because the aide might otherwise record superficial or inadequate answers if he does not fully understand the questions
D. *inadvisable*, because the information obtained through the form may be of little importance to the aide

16. Which one of the following is NOT a general accepted rule of telephone etiquette for an administrative aide? 16.____

A. Answer the telephone as soon as possible after the first ring
B. Speak in a louder than normal tone of voice, on the assumption that the caller is hard-of-hearing
C. Have a pencil and paper ready at all times with which to make notes and take messages
D. Use the tone of your voice to give the caller the impression of cooperativeness and willingness to be of service

17. The one of the following which is the BEST reason for placing the date and time of receipt of incoming mail is that this procedure 17.____
   A. aids the filing of correspondence in alphabetical order
   B. fixes responsibility for promptness in answering correspondence
   C. indicates that the mail has been checked for the presence of a return address
   D. makes it easier to distribute the mail in sequence

18. Which one of the following is the FIRST step that you should take when filing a document by subject? 18.____
   A. Arrange related documents by date with the latest date in front
   B. Check whether the document has been released for filing
   C. Cross-reference the document if necessary
   D. Determine the category under which the document will be filed

19. The one of the following which is NOT generally employed to keep tract of frequently used material requiring future attention is a 19.____
   A. card tickler file
   B. dated follow-up folder
   C. periodic transferral of records
   D. signal folder

20. Assume that a newly appointed administrative aide arrives 15 minutes late for the start of his tour of duty. One of his co-workers tells him not to worry because he has signed him in on time. The co-worker assures him that he would be willing to over for him anytime he is late and hopes the aide will do the same for him. The aide agrees to do so. 20.____
This arrangement is
   A. *desirable*; it prevents both men from getting a record for tardiness
   B. *undesirable*; signing in for each other is dishonest
   C. *desirable*; cooperation among co-workers is an important factor in morale
   D. *undesirable*; they will get caught if one is held up in a lengthy delay

21. An administrative aide takes great pains to help a citizen who approaches him with a problem. The citizen thanks the aide curtly and without enthusiasm. Under these circumstances, it would be MOST courteous for the aide to 21.____
   A. tell the citizen he was glad to be of service
   B. ask the citizen to put the compliment into writing and send it to his supervisor
   C. tell the citizen just what pains he took to render this service so that the citizen will be fully aware of his efforts
   D. make no reply and ignore the citizen's remarks

22. Assume that your supervisor spends a week training you, a newly appointed administrative aide, to sort fingerprint for filing purposes. After doing this type of filing for several day, you get an idea which you believe would improve upon the method in use. 22.____
Of the following, the BEST action for you to take in this situation is to
   A. wait to see whether your idea still look good after you have had more experience
   B. try your idea out before bringing it up with your supervisor

C. discuss your idea with your supervisor
D. forget about this idea since the fingerprint sorting system was devised by experts

23. Which one of the following is NOT a useful filing practice? 23.____
A. Filing active records in the most accessible parts of the file cabinet
B. Filling a file drawer to capacity in order to save space
C. Gluing small documents to standard-size paper before filing
D. Using different colored tab for various filing categories

24. A citizen comes in to make a complaint to an administrative aide. 24.____
The one of the following action which would be the MOST serious example of discourtesy would be for the aide to
A. refuse to look up from his desk even though he knows someone is waiting to speak to him
B. not use the citizen's name when addressing him once his identity has been ascertained
C. interrupt the citizen's story to ask questions
D. listen to the complaint and refer the citizen to a special office

25. Suppose that one of your neighbors walks into the precinct where you are an administrative aide and asks you to make 100 copies of a letter on the office duplicating machine for his personal use. 25.____
Of the following, what action should you take FIRST in this situation?
A. Pretend that you do not know the person and order him to leave the building
B. Call a police officer and report the person for attempting to make illegal use of police equipment
C. Tell the person that you will copy the letter but only when you are off-duty
D. Explain to the person that you cannot use police equipment for non-police work

KEY (CORRECT ANSWERS)

1. C
2. A
3. A
4. C
5. B

6. C
7. A
8. B
9. D
10. D

11. D
12. C
13. A
14. C
15. C

16. B
17. B
18. B
19. C
20. B

21. A
22. C
23. B
24. A
25. D

TEST 2

DIRECTIONS: Each question or incomplete statement is followed by several suggested answers or completions. Select the one that BEST answers the question or completes the statement. *PRINT THE LETTER OF THE CORRECT ANSWER IN THE SPACE AT THE RIGHT.*

Questions 1-6.

DIRECTIONS: Questions 1 through 6 are to be answered on the basis of the information supplied in the chart below.

LAW ENFORCEMENT OFFICERS KILLED
(By Type of Activity)
2012-2021

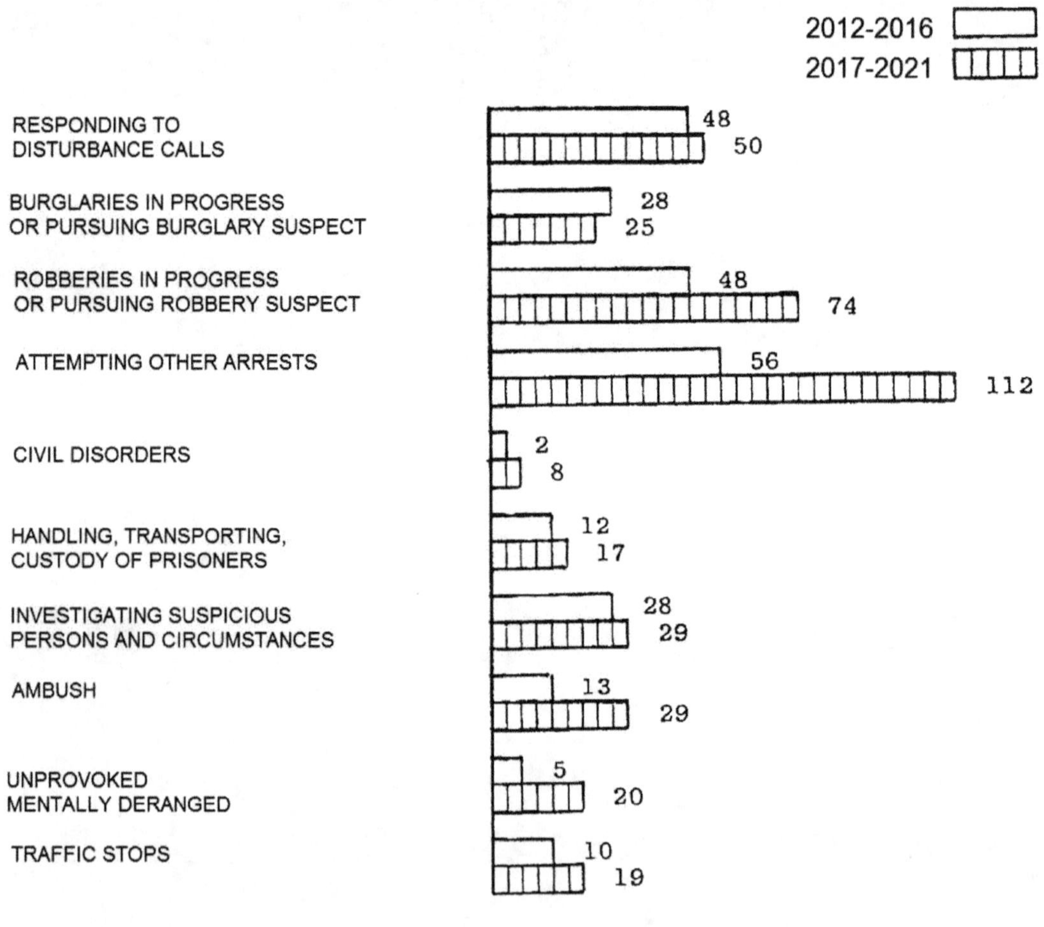

1. According to the above chart, the percent of the total number of law enforcement officers killed from 2012-2021 in activities related to burglaries and robberies is MOST NEARLY _____ percent. 1.____
   A. 8.4 B. 19.3 C. 27.6 D. 36.2

2. According to the above chart, the two of the following categories which increased from 2012–16 to 2017–21 by the same percent are 2.____
   A. ambush and traffic stops
   B. attempting other arrests and ambush
   C. civil disorders and unprovoked mentally deranged
   D. response to disturbance calls and investigating suspicious persons and circumstances

3. According to the above chart, the percentage increase in law enforcement officers killed from the 2012-16 period to the 2017-21 period is MOST NEARLY _____ percent. 3.____
   A. 34 B. 53 C. 65 D. 100

4. According to the above chart, in which one of the following activities did the number of law enforcement officers killed increase by 100 percent? 4.____
   A. Ambush
   B. Attempting other arrests
   C. Robberies in progress or pursuing robbery suspect
   D. Traffic stops

5. According to the above chart, the two of the following activities during which the total number of law enforcement officers killed from 2012 to 2021 was the same are 5.____
   A. burglaries in progress or pursuing burglary suspect and investigating suspicious persons and circumstances
   B. handling, transporting, custody of prisoner and traffic stops
   C. investigating suspicious persons and circumstances and ambush
   D. responding to disturbance calls and robberies in progress or pursuing robbery suspect

6. According to the categories in the above chart, the one of the following statements which can be made about law enforcement officers killed from 2012 to 2016 is that 6.____
   A. the number of law enforcement officers killed during civil disorders equals one-sixth of the number killed responding to disturbance calls
   B. the number of law enforcement officers killed during robberies in progress or pursuing robbery suspect equals 25 percent of the number killed while handling or transporting prisoners
   C. the number of law enforcement officers killed during traffic stops equals one-half the number killed for unprovoked reasons or by the mentally deranged
   D. twice as many law enforcement officers were killed attempting other arrests as were killed during burglaries in progress or pursuing burglary suspect

Questions 7-10.

DIRECTIONS: Assume that all arrests fall into two mutually exclusive categories, felonies and misdemeanors. Last week 620 arrests were made in Precinct A, of which 403 were for felonies. Questions 7 through 10 are to be answered on the basis of this information.

7. The percent of all arrests made in Precinct A last week which were for felonies was _____ percent. 7.____
   A. 55 B. 60 C. 65 D. 70

8. If 3/5 of all persons arrested for felonies and 1/4 of all persons arrested for misdemeanors were carrying weapons, then the number of arrests involving persons carrying weapons in Precinct A last week was MOST NEARLY 8.____
   A. 135 B. 295 C. 415 D. 525

9. If five times as many men as women were arrested for felonies, and half as many women as men were arrested for misdemeanors, then the number of women arrested in Precinct A last week was APPROXIMATELY 9.____
   A. 90 B. 120 C. 175 D. 210

10. If the ratio of arrests made on weekends (Friday through Sunday) to arrests made on weekdays (Monday through Thursday) is 2:1, then the number of arrests made in Precinct A last weekend was 10.____
   A. 308 B. 340 C. 372 D. 413

11. The police precincts covering the county receive calls at the average rate of two per minute during the 8 A.M. to 4 P.M. tour, but this rate increases by 50 percent during the 4 P.M. to 12 A.M. tour. However, the initial rate decreases by 50 percent during the 12 A.M. to 8 A.M. tour. 11.____
   The number of calls received by the precincts covering the county on this basis is one 24-hour day is
   A. 960 B. 1,440 C. 2,880 D. 3,360

12. If an administrative aide is expected to handle 15 calls per hour and Precinct C averages 840 calls during the 4 P.M. to 12 A.M. tour, then the number of aides needed in Precinct C to handle calls during this tour is 12.____
   A. 4 B. 5 C. 6 D. 7

13. If in a group of ten administrative aides, four type 40 words per minute, one types 45, two type 50, two type 60, and one types 65, then the average speed in the group is 13.____
   A. 49 B. 50 C. 51 D. 52

14. An administrative aide works from midnight to 8 A.M. on a certain day and then is off for 64 hours. 14.____
   He is due back at work at
   A. 8 A.M. B. 12 noon C. 4 P.M. D. 12 midnight

15. If a certain aide take one hour to type 2 accident reports or 6 missing person reports, then the length of time he will require to finish 7 accident reports and 15 missing persons reports is _____ hours _____ minutes. 15.____
   A. 6; 0 B. 6; 30 C. 8; 0 D. 8; 40

16. If one administrative aide can alphabetize 320 reports per hour and another can do 280 per hour, then the number of reports that both could alphabetize during an 8-hour tour is 16.____
   A. 4,800 B. 5,200 C. 5,400 D. 5,700

17. If 1,000 candidates applied for administrative aide, and out of those applying 7/8 appear for the written test, and out of those who take the written test 66 2/4 percent pass it, and out of those who pass the written test 85 percent pass the medical exam, then the number of candidates still eligible to become administrative aides will be about 17.____
   A. 245 B. 495 C. 585 D. 745

18. If the number of murders in the city in 2018 was 415, and the number of murders has increased by 8 percent each year since that year, then in 2021 we would expect the number of murders to be about 18.____
   A. 484 B. 523 C. 548 D. 565

19. If a person reported missing on April 15 was found murdered on July 4, how many days was he missing? (Include April 15 but NOT July 4 in the total.) 19.____
   A. 76 B. 80 C. 82 D. 84

20. Suppose that a pile of 96 file cards measures one inch in height and that it takes you ½ hour to file these cards away.
If you are given three piles of cards which measure 2½ inches high, 1¾ inches high, and $3^3/_8$ inches high, respectfully, the time it would take to file the cards is MOST NEARLY _____ hours and _____ minutes. 20.____
   A. 2; 30 B. 3; 50 C. 6; 45 D. 8; 15

Questions 21-30.

DIRECTIONS: Questions 21 through 30 test how good you are at catching mistakes in typing or printing. In each question, the name and addresses in Column II should be an exact copy of the name and address in Column I.
Mark your answer:
A. if there is no mistake in either name or address
B. if there is a mistake in both name and address
C. if there is a mistake only in the name
D. if there is a mistake only in the address

	COLUMN I	COLUMN II	
21.	Milos Yanocek 33-60 14 Street Long Island City, NY 11011	Milos Yanocek 33-60 14 Street Long Island City, NY 11001	21.____

22.	Alphonse Sabattelo 24 Minnetta Lane New York, NY 10006	Alphonse Sabbattelo 24 Minetta Lane New York, NY 10006	22.____
23.	Helen Stearn 5 Metroplitan Oval Bronx, NY 10462	Helene Steam 5 Metropolitan Oval Bronx, NY 10462	23.____
24.	Jacob Weisman 231 Francis Lewis Boulevard Forest Hills, NY 11325	Jacob Weisman 231 Francis Lewis Boulevard Forest Hill, NY 11325	24.____
25.	Riccardo Fuente 135 West 83 Street New York, NY 10024	Riccardo Fuentes 134 West 88 Street New York, NY 10024	25.____
26.	Dennis Lauber 52 Avenue D Brooklyn, NY 11216	Dennis Lauder 52 Avenue D Brooklyn, NY 11216	26.____
27.	Paul Cutter 195 Galloway Avenue Staten Island, NY 10356	Paul Cutter 175 Galloway Avenue Staten Island, NY 10365	27.____
28.	Sean Donnelly 45-58 41 Avenue Woodside, NY 11168	Sean Donnelly 45-58 41 Avenue Woodside, NY 11168	28.____
29.	Clyde Willot 1483 Rockaway Avenue Brooklyn, NY 11238	Clyde Willat 1483 Rockaway Avenue Brooklyn, NY 11238	29.____
30.	Michael Stanakis 419 Sheriden Avenue Staten Island, NY 10363	Michael Stanakis 419 Sheraden Avenue Staten Island, NY 10363	30.____

Questions 31-40.

DIRECTIONS: Questions 31 through 40 are to be answered SOLELY on the basis of the following information.

Column I consists of serial numbers of dollar bills. Column II shows different ways of arranging the corresponding serial numbers.

The serial numbers of dollar bills in Column I begin and end with a capital letter and have an eight-digit number in between. The serial numbers in Column I are to be arranged according to the following rules:

First: In alphabetical order according to the first letter.
Second: When two or more serial numbers have the same first letter, in alphabetical order according to the last letter.
Third: When two or more serial numbers have the same first and last letters, in numerical order, beginning with the lowest number.

The serial numbers in Column I are numbered (1) through (5) in the order in which they are listed. In Column II, the numbers (1) through (5) are arranged in four different ways to show different arrangements of the corresponding serial numbers. Choose the answer in Column II in which the serial numbers are arranged according to the above rules.
SAMPLE QUESTION:

COLUMN I		COLUMN II	
(1)	E75044127B	(A)	4, 1, 3, 2, 5
(2)	B96399104A	(B)	4, 1 2, 3, 5
(3)	B93939086A	(C)	4, 3, 2 5, 1
(4)	B47064465H	(D)	3, 2, 5, 4, 1
(5)	B99040922A		

In the sample question, the four serial numbers starting with B should be put before the serial numbers starting with E. The serial numbers starting with B and ending with A should be put before the serial number starting with B and ending with H. The three serial numbers starting with B and ending with A should be listed in numerical order, beginning with the lowest number. The correct way to arrange the serial numbers, therefore, is

(3) B93939086A
(2) B96399104A
(5) B99040922A
(4) B47064465H
(1) B75044127B

Since the order of arrangement is 3, 2, 5, 4, 1, the answer to the sample question is (D).

	COLUMN I		COLUMN II		
31.	(1) P44343324Y	A.	2, 3, 1, 4, 5		31.____
	(2) P44141341S	B.	1, 5, 3, 2, 4		
	(3) P44141431L	C.	4, 2, 3, 5, 1		
	(4) P41143413W	D.	5, 3, 2, 4, 1		
	(5) P44313433H				
32.	(1) D89077275M	A.	3, 2, 5, 3, 1		32.____
	(2) D98073724N	B.	1, 4, 3, 2, 5		
	(3) D90877274N	C.	4, 1, 5, 2, 3		
	(4) D98877275M	D.	1, 3, 2, 5, 3		
	(5) D98873725N				

33. (1) H32548137E (2) H35243178A (3) H35284378F (4) H35288337A (5) H32883173B
A. 2, 4, 5, 1, 3
B. 1, 5, 2, 3, 4
C. 1, 5, 2, 4, 3
D. 2, 1, 5, 3, 4
33.____

34. (1) K24165039H (2) F24106599A (3) L21406639G (4) C24156093A (5) K24165593D
A. 4, 2, 5, 3, 1
B. 2, 3, 4, 1, 5
C. 4, 2, 5, 1, 3
D. 1, 3, 4, 5, 2
34.____

35. (1) H79110642E (2) H79101928E (3) A79111567F (4) H79111796E (5) A79111618F
A. 2, 1, 3, 5, 4
B. 2, 1, 4, 5, 3
C. 3, 5, 2, 1, 4
D. 4, 3, 5, 1, 2
35.____

36. (1) P16388385W (2) R16388335V (3) P16383835W (4) R18386865V (5) P18686865W
A. 3, 4, 5, 2, 1
B. 2, 3, 4, 5, 1
C. 2, 4, 3, 1, 5
D. 3, 1, 5, 2, 4
36.____

37. (1) B42271749G (2) B42271779G (3) E43217779G (4) B42874119C (5) E42817749G
A. 4, 1, 5, 2, 3
B. 4, 1, 2, 5, 3
C. 1, 2, 4, 5, 3
D. 5, 3, 1, 2, 4
37.____

38. (1) M57906455S (2) N87077758S (3) N87707757B (4) M57877759B (5) M57906555S
A. 4, 1, 5, 3, 2
B. 3, 4, 1, 5, 2
C. 4, 1, 5, 2, 3
D. 1, 5, 3, 2, 4
38.____

39. (1) C69336894Y (2) C69336684V (3) C69366887W (4) C69366994Y (5) C69336865V
A. 2, 5, 3, 1, 4
B. 3, 2, 5, 1, 4
C. 3, 1, 4, 5, 2
D. 2, 5, 1, 3, 4
39.____

40. (1) A56247181D (2) A56272128P (3) H56247128D (4) H56272288P (5) A56247188D
A. 1, 5, 3, 2, 4
B. 3, 1, 5, 2, 4
C. 3, 2, 1, 5, 4
D. 1, 5, 2, 3, 4
40.____

Questions 41-48.

DIRECTIONS: Questions 41 through 48 are to be answered SOLELY on the basis of the following passage.

Auto theft is prevalent and costly. In 2020, 486,000 autos valued at over $500 million were stolen. About 28 percent of the inhabitants of federal prisons are there as a result of conviction of interstate auto theft under the Dyer Act. In California alone, auto thefts cost the criminal justice system approximately $60 million yearly.

The great majority of auto theft is for temporary use rather than resale, as evidenced by the fact that 88 percent of autos stolen in 2020 were recovered. In Los Angeles, 64 percent of stolen autos that were recovered were found within two days and about 80 percent within a week. Chicago reports that 71 percent of the recovered autos were found within four miles of the point of theft. The FBI estimates that 8 percent of stolen cars are taken for the purpose of stripping them for parts, 12 percent for resale, and 5 percent for use in another crime. Auto thefts are primarily juvenile acts. Although only 21 percent of all arrests for nontraffic offenses in 2020 were of individuals under 18 years of age, 63 percent of auto theft arrests were of persons under 18. Auto theft represents the start of many criminal careers; in an FBI sample of juvenile auto theft offenders, 41 percent had no prior arrest record.

41. In the above passage, the discussion of the reasons for auto theft does NOT include the percent of 41.____
   A. autos stolen by prior offenders
   B. recovered stolen autos found close to the point of theft
   C. stolen autos recovered within a week
   D. stolen autos which were recovered

42. Assuming the figures in the above passage remain constant, you may logically estimate the cost of auto thefts to the California criminal justice system over a five-year period beginning in 2020 to have been about _____ million. 42.____
   A. $200 B. $300 C. $440 D. $500

43. According to the above passage, the percent of stolen autos in Los Angeles which were not recovered within a week was _____ percent. 43.____
   A. 12 B. 20 C. 29 D. 36

44. According to the above passage, MOST auto thefts are committed by 44.____
   A. former inmates of federal prisons
   B. juveniles
   C. persons with a prior arrest record
   D. residents of large cities

45. According to the above passage, MOST autos are stolen for 45.____
   A. resale
   B. stripping of parts
   C. temporary use
   D. use in another crime

46. According to the above passage, the percent of persons arrested for auto theft who were under 18 46.____
   A. equals nearly the same percent of stolen autos which were recovered
   B. equals nearly two-thirds of the total number of persons arrested for nontraffic offenses
   C. is the same as the percent of persons arrested for nontraffic offenses who were under 18
   D. is three times the percent of persons arrested for nontraffic offenses who were under 18

47. An APPROPRIATE title for the above passage is 47.____
   A. How Criminal Careers Begin
   B. Recovery of Stolen Cars
   C. Some Statistics on Auto Theft
   D. The Costs of Auto Theft

48. Based on the above passage, the number of cars taken for use in another crime in 2020 was 48.____
   A. 24,300
   B. 38,880
   C. 48,600
   D. 58,320

Questions 49-55.

DIRECTIONS: Questions 49 through 55 are to be answered SOLELY on the basis of the following passage.

Burglar alarms are designed to detect intrusion automatically. Robbery alarms enable a victim of a robbery or an attack to signal for help. Such devices can be located in elevators, hallways, homes and apartments, businesses and factories, and subways, as well as on the street in high-crime areas. Alarms could deter some potential criminals from attacking targets so protected. If alarms were prevalent and not visible, then they might serve to suppress crime generally. In addition, of course, the alarms can summon the police when they are needed.

All alarms must perform three functions: sensing or initiation of the signal, transmission of the signal, and annunciation of the alarm. A burglar alarm needs a sensor to detect human presence or activity in an unoccupied enclosed area like a building or a room. A robbery victim would initiate the alarm by closing a foot or wall switch, or by triggering a portable transmitter which would send the alarm signal to a remote receiver. The signal can sound locally as a loud noise to frighten away a criminal, or it can be sent silently by wire to a central agency. A centralized annunciator requires either private lines from each alarmed point, or the transmission of some information on the location of the signal.

49. A conclusion which follows LOGICALLY from the above passage is that 49.____
   A. burglar alarms employ sensor devices; robbery alarms make use of initiation devices
   B. robbery alarms signal intrusion without the help of the victim; burglar alarms require the victim to trigger a switch
   C. robbery alarms sound locally; burglar alarms are transmitted to a central agency
   D. the mechanisms for a burglar alarm and a robbery alarm are alike

50. According to the above passage, alarms can be located 50.____
   A. in a wide variety of settings
   B. only in enclosed areas
   C. at low cost in high-crime areas
   D. only in places where potential criminal will be deterred

51. According to the above passage, which of the following is ESSENTIAL if a signal is to be received in a central office? 51.____
   A. A foot or wall switch
   B. A noise producing mechanism
   C. A portable reception device
   D. Information regarding the location of the source

52. According to the above passage, an alarm system can function WITHOUT a 52.____
   A. centralized annunciating device
   B. device to stop the alarm
   C. sensing or initiating device
   D. transmission device

53. According to the above passage, the purpose of robbery alarms is to 53.____
   A. find out automatically whether a robbery has taken place
   B. lower the crime rate in high-crime areas
   C. make a loud noise to frighten away the criminal
   D. provide a victim with the means to signal for help

54. According to the above passage, alarms might aid in lessening crime if they were 54.____
   A. answered promptly by police
   B. completely automatic
   C. easily accessible to victims
   D. hidden and widespread

55. Of the following, the BEST title for the above passage is 55.____
   A. Detection of Crime By Alarms
   B. Lowering the Crime Rate
   C. Suppression of Crime
   D. The Prevention of Robbery

KEY (CORRECT ANSWERS)

1.	C	11.	C	21.	D	31.	D	41.	A	51.	D
2.	C	12.	D	22.	B	32.	B	42.	B	52.	A
3.	B	13.	A	23.	C	33.	A	43.	B	53.	D
4.	B	14.	D	24.	A	34.	C	44.	B	54.	D
5.	B	15.	A	25.	B	35.	C	45.	C	55.	A
6.	D	16.	A	26.	C	36.	D	46.	D		
7.	C	17.	B	27.	D	37.	B	47.	C		
8.	B	18.	B	28.	A	38.	A	48.	A		
9.	C	19.	B	29.	B	39.	A	49.	A		
10.	D	20.	B	30.	D	40.	D	50.	A		

EXAMINATION SECTION

TEST 1

DIRECTIONS: Each question or incomplete statement is followed by several suggested answers or completions. Select the one that BEST answers the question or completes the statement. *PRINT THE LETTER OF THE CORRECT ANSWER IN THE SPACE AT THE RIGHT.*

1. As an administrative aide, it is your job to type reports prepared by several police officers. These reports are then returned to them for review and signature. Officer X consistently submits reports to you which contain misspellings and incorrect punctuation. 1.____
   Of the following, the BEST action for you to take is to
   A. tell your supervisor that something must be done about Officer X's poor English
   B. ask Officer X for permission to correct any mistakes
   C. assemble all of the officers and tell them that you refuse to correct their mistakes
   D. tell Officer X to be more careful

2. On a chart used in your precinct, there appear small figures of men, women, and children to denote population trends. Your supervisor assigns you to suggest possible symbols for a char which will be used to indicate daily vehicular traffic flow in the area covered by this precinct. 2.____
   In this situation, your BEST course of action would be to
   A. tell your supervisor an artist should be hired to draw these symbols
   B. make up a list of possible symbols, such as cars and trucks
   C. say that any decision as to the symbols to be used should be made at a higher level
   D. find out how many vehicles use the area

3. As an administrative aide, you are assigned to the telephone switchboard. An extremely irate citizen calls complaining in bigoted terms about a group of Black teenagers who congregate in front of his house. The caller insists on speaking to whoever is in charge. At the moment, Sergeant X, a black man, is in charge. 3.____
   The BEST course of action for you to take is to
   A. inform the caller that the teenagers may meet wherever they wish
   B. tell the caller that Sergeant X, a black man, is in charge, and ask him to call back later when a white man will be there
   C. tell the caller that you resent his bigotry and insist that he call back when he has calmed down
   D. acquaint Sergeant X with the circumstances and connect the caller with him

4. Assume that you have access to restricted materials such as conviction records. A friend asks you, unofficially, if a man he has recently met has a record of conviction. 4.____
The BEST thing for you to do is to
   A. give your friend the information he wants and inform your supervisor of your actions
   B. tell your friend that you are not allowed to give out such information
   C. tell your friend you will try to get the information for him but do not take any action
   D. give him the information because it is a matter of public record

5. Assume that you are an administrative aide assigned to a busy telephone information center. 5.____
Of the following, which is the MOST important technique to use when answering the telephone?
   A. Using many technical police terms
   B. Speaking slowly, in a monotone, for clarity
   C. Using formal English grammar
   D Speaking clearly and distinctly

6. As an administrative aide, you are asked by an officer working in an adjacent office to type a very important letter without mistakes or corrections exactly as he has prepared it. As you are typing, you notice a word which, according to the dictionary, is misspelled. 6.____
Under the circumstances, you should
   A. ignore the error and type it exactly as prepared
   B. change the spelling without telling the officer
   C. ask the officer if you should change the spelling
   D. change the spelling and tell the officer

7. As am administrative aide, you are in charge of a large complex of files. In an effort to be helpful, some officers who frequently use the file have begun to refile material they had been using. Unfortunately, they often make errors. 7.____
Of the following, your BEST course of action is to
   A. ask them to leave the files for you to put away
   B. ask your supervisor to reprimand them
   C. frequently check the whole filing system for errors
   D. tell them they are making mistakes and insist they leave the files alone

8. One afternoon several of the police officers ask you to do different tasks. Each task will take about a day to complete, but each officer insists that his work must be completed immediately. 8.____
Your BEST course of action is to
   A. do a little of each assignment given to you
   B. ask your fellow workers to help you with the assignment
   C. speak to your supervisor in order to determine the priority of the assignments
   D. do the work in the order of the rank of the officers giving the assignments

Questions 9-12.

DIRECTIONS: Questions 9 through 12 are to be answered on the basis of the following passage.

It should be emphasized that one goal of law enforcement is the reduction of stress between one population group and another. When no stress exists between populations, law enforcement can deal with other tensions or simply perform traditional police functions. However, when stress between populations does exist, law enforcement, in its efforts to prevent disruptive behavior, becomes committed to reducing that stress (if for no other reason than its responsibility to maintain an orderly environment). The type of stress to be reduced, unlike the tension stemming from social change, is stress generated through intergroup and interracial friction. Of course, all sources of tension are inextricably interrelated, but friction between different populations in the community is of immediate concern to law enforcement.

9. The above passage emphasizes that, during times of stress between groups in the community, it is necessary for the police to attempt to 9.____
   A. continue their traditional duties
   B. eliminate tension resulting from social change
   C. reduce intergroup stress
   D. punish disruptive behavior

10. Based on the above passage, police concern with tension among groups in a community is MOST likely to stem primarily from their desire to 10.____
   A. establish racial justice
   B. prevent violence
   C. protect property
   D. unite the diverse groups

11. According to the above passage, enforcers of the law are responsible for 11.____
   A. analyzing consequences of population-group hostility
   B. assisting social work activities
   C. creating order in the environment
   D. explaining group behavior

12. The factor which produces the tension accompanying social change is 12.____
   A. a disorderly environment
   B. disruptive behavior
   C. inter-community hostility
   D. not discussed in the above passage

Questions 13-19.

DIRECTIONS: Questions 13 through 19 are to be answered on the basis of the information given in the following passage.

From a nationwide point of view, the need for new housing units during the years immediately ahead will be determined by four major factors. The most important factor is the net change in household formations—that is, the difference between the number of new households that are formed and the number of existing households that are dissolved, whether by death or other circumstances. During the 1990's, as the children born during the decades of the 60's and 70's come of age and marry, the total number of households is expected to increase at a rate of more than 1,000,000 annually. The second factor affecting the need for new housing units is *removals*—that is, existing units that are demolished, damaged beyond repair, or otherwise removed from the housing supply. A third factor is the number of existing vacancies. To some extent, vacancies can satisfy the housing demand caused by increases in total number of households or by removals, although population shifts that are already under way mean that some areas will have a surfeit of vacancies and other areas will be faced with serious shortages of housing. A final factor, and one that has only recently assumed major importance, is the increasing demand for second homes. These may take any form from a shack in the woods for the city dweller to a *pied-a-terre* in the city for a suburbanite. Whatever the form, however, it is certain that increasing leisure time, rising amounts of discretionary income, and improvements in transportation are leading more and more Americans to look on a second home not as a rich man's luxury but as the common man's right.

13. The above passage uses the term *housing units* to refer to 13.____
    A. residences of all kinds
    B. apartment buildings only
    C. one-family houses only
    D. the total number of families in the United States

14. The passage uses the word *removals* to mean 14.____
    A. the shift of population from one area to another
    B. vacancies that occur when families move
    C. financial losses suffered when a building is damaged or destroyed
    D. former dwellings that are demolished or can no longer be used for housing

15. The expression *pied-a-terre* appears in the next-to-last sentence in the passage. A person who is not familiar with the expression should be able to tell from the way it is used here that it probably means 15.____
    A. a suburban home owned by a commuter
    B. a shack in the woods
    C. a second home that is used from time to time
    D. overnight lodging for a traveler in a strange city

16. Of the factors described in the passage as having an important influence on the demand for housing, which factor—taken alone—is LEAST likely to encourage the construction of new housing? 16.____
    The
    A. net change in household formations
    B. destruction of existing housing
    C. existence of vacancies
    D. use of second homes

17. Based on the above passage, the TOTAL increase in the number of households during the 1990's is expected to be MOST NEARLY 17.____
    A. 1,000,000 B. 10,000,000
    C. 100,000,000 D. 1,000,000,000

18. Which one of the following conclusions could MOST logically be drawn from the information given in the passage? 18.____
   A. The population of the United States is increasing at the rate of about 1,000,000 people annually.
   B. There is already a severe housing shortage in all parts of the country.
   C. The need for additional housing units is greater in some parts of the country than in others.
   D. It is still true that only wealthy people can afford to keep up more than one home.

19. Which one of the following conclusions could NOT logically be drawn from the information given in the passage? 19.____
   A. The need for new housing will be even greater in the 2000's than in the 1990's.
   B. Demolition of existing housing must be taken into account in calculating the need for new housing construction.
   C. Having a second home is more common today than it was in the 1960's.
   D. Part of the housing needs of the 1990's can be met by vacancies.

20. You are making a report on the number of incoming calls handled by two different switchboards. Over a five-day period, the total count of incoming calls per day for both switchboards together was 2,773. The average number of incoming calls per day for Switchboard A was 301. You cannot find one day's tally for Switchboard B, but the total for the other four days for Switchboard B come to 1,032. 20.____
Determine from this how many incoming calls must have been reported on the *missing* tally for Switchboard B.
   A. 236 B. 259 C. 408 D. 1,440

21. Assume that one-page notices for distribution may be reproduced by photocopy or by a designer. The cost for photocopying is 5½ cents per copy. It can also be reproduced by a designer for an initial preparation cost of $1.38 plus a per-copy cost of one cent. 21.____
Strictly according to cost, which of the following is the LOWEST number of copies at which it would be more economical to choose the designer instead of photocopying?
   A. 15 B. 30 C. 45 D. 138

22. An employee completed 75% of a clerical assignment in four days. 22.____
How much of it did he complete in the last two days if he finished 3/8 of it in the first two days?
   A. 1/4 B. 3/8 C. 5/8 D. 3/4

23. Seven hundred people are to be scheduled for interviews. 23.____
If 58% of these 700 people have already been scheduled, how many more must be scheduled?
   A. 138 B. 294 C. 406 D. 410

24. In recent years, an average of 35% of the violations reported in any given month have been corrected by the time of a follow-up inspection one month later. Last month, 240 violations were reported, and this month's follow-up inspections show that 93 of them have been corrected. How many more violations have been corrected than would have been expected based on the average rate? 24.____
A. 5 B. 9 C. 33 D. 58

25. Suppose that, on a scaled drawing of an office floor plan, ½ inch equals 2 feet. An office that is actually 12 feet wide and 17 feet long has which of the following dimensions on this scaled drawing? 25.____
_____ wide and _____.
A. 3"; 4.25" B. 6"' 8.5" C. 12"; 17" D. 24"; 34"

KEY (CORRECT ANSWERS)

1. B
2. B
3. D
4. B
5. D

6. C
7. A
8. C
9. C
10. B

11. C
12. D
13. A
14. D
15. C

16. C
17. B
18. C
19. A
20. A

21. C
22. B
23. B
24. B
25. A

TEST 2

DIRECTIONS: Each question or incomplete statement is followed by several suggested answers or completions. Select the one that BEST answers the question or completes the statement. *PRINT THE LETTER OF THE CORRECT ANSWER IN THE SPACE AT THE RIGHT.*

1. Suppose that employees in a certain division put in a total of 1,250 hours of overtime in 2019. In 2020, total overtime hours for the same division were 2% less than in 2019, but in 2021 overtime hours increased by 8% over the 2020 total. 1.____
   How many overtime hours were worked by the staff of this division in 2021?
   A. 1,323 B. 1,331 C. 1,350 D. 1,375

2. A particular operation currently involves 75 employees, 80% of whom work in the field and the rest of whom are office staff. A management study has shown that in order to be truly efficient, the operation should have a ratio of at least 1 office employee to every 3 field employees, and the study recommends that the number of field employees remain the same as at present. 2.____
   What is the MINIMUM number of employees needed to carry out the operation efficiently, according to this recommendation?
   A. 65 B. 75 C. 80 D. 100

Questions 3-6.

DIRECTIONS: Questions 3 through 6 are to be answered on the basis of the information given in the following passage.

Data processing is by no means a new invention. In one form or another, it has been carried on throughout the entire history of civilization. In its most general sense, data processing means organizing data so that it can be used for a specific purpose, a procedure commonly known simply as *record-keeping* or paperwork. With the development of modern office equipment, and particularly with the recent introduction of computers, the techniques of data processing have become highly elaborate and sophisticated, but the basic purpose remains the same: turning raw data into useful information.

The key concept here is usefulness. The data, or input, that is to be processed can be compared to the raw material that is to go into a manufacturing process. The information, or output, that results from data processing—like the finished product of a manufacturer—should be clearly usable. A collection of data has little value unless it is converted into information that serves a specific function.

3. The expression *paperwork*, as it is used in this passage, 3.____
   A. shows that the author regards such operations as a waste of time
   B. has the same general meaning as *data processing*
   C. refers to methods of record-keeping that are no longer in use
   D. indicates that the public does not understand the purpose of data processing

4. The passage indicates that the use of computers has 4.____
   A. greatly simplified the clerical work in an office
   B. led to more complicated systems for the handling of data
   C. had no effect whatsoever on data processing
   D. made other modern office machines obsolete

5. Which of the following BEST expresses the basic principle of data processing as it is described in the passage? 5.____
   A. Input – processing – output
   B. Historical record-keeping – modern techniques – specific functions
   C. Office equipment – computer – accurate data
   D. Raw material – manufacturer - retailer

6. According to the above passage, data processing may be described as 6.____
   A. a new management technique
   B. computer technology
   C. information output
   D. record-keeping

Questions 7-10.

DIRECTIONS: Questions 7 through 10 are to be answered on the basis of the following passage.

Analysis of current data reveals that motor vehicle transportation actually requires less space than was used for other types of transportation in the pre-automobile era, even including the substantial area taken by freeways. The reason is that when the fast-moving through traffic is put on built-for-the-purpose arterial roads, then the amount of ordinary space needed for strictly local movement and for access to property drops sharply. Even the amount of land taken for urban expressways turns out to be surprisingly small in terms either of total urban acreage or of the volume of traffic they carry. No existing or contemplated urban expressway system requires as much as 3 percent of the land in the areas it serves, and this would be exceptionally high. The Los Angeles freeway system, when complete, will occupy only 2 percent of the available land; the same is true of the District of Columbia, where only 0.75 percent will be pavement, with the remaining 1.25 percent as open space. California studies estimate that, in a typical California urban community, 1.6 to 2 percent of the area should be devoted to freeways, which will handle 50 to 60 percent of all traffic needs, and about ten times as much land to the ordinary roads and streets that carry the rest of the traffic. By comparison, when John A. Sutter laid out Sacramento in 1850, he provided 38 percent of the area for streets and sidewalks. The French architect, Pierre L'Enfant, proposed 59 percent of the area of the District of Columbia for roads and streets; urban renewal in Southwest Washington, incorporating a modern street network, reduced the acreage of space for pedestrian and vehicular traffic in the renewal area from 48.2 to 41.5 percent of the total. If we are to have a reasonable consideration of the impact of highway transportation on contemporary urban development, it would be well to understand these relationships.

7. The author of this passage says that 7.____
   A. modern transportation uses less space than was used for transportation before the auto age
   B. expressways require more space than streets in terms of urban acreage

C. typical urban communities were poorly designed in terms of relationship between space used for traffic and that used for other purposes
D. the need for local and access roads would increase if the number of expressways were increased

8. According to the above passage, it was originally planned that the percent of the area to be used for roads and streets in the District of Columbia should be MOST NEARLY 8.____
A. 40% B. 45% C. 505 D. 60%

9. The above passage states that the amount of space needed for local traffic 9.____
A. *increases* when arterial highways are constructed
B. *decreases* when arterial highways are constructed
C. *decreases* when there is more land available
D. *increases* when there is more land available

10. According to the above passage, studies estimate that, in a typical California urban community, the amount of land devoted to ordinary roads and streets as compared with that devoted to freeways should be MOST NEARLY _____ as much. 10.____
A. one-half B. one-tenth C. twice D. ten times

Questions 11-13.

DIRECTIONS: Questions 11 through 13 are to be answered on the basis of the following passage.

A glaring exception to the usual practice of the judicial trial as a means of conflict resolution is the utilization of administrative hearings. The growing tendency to create administrative bodies with rule-making and quasi-judicial powers has shattered many standard concepts. A comprehensive examination of the legal process cannot neglect these newer patterns.

In the administrative process, the legislative, executive, and judicial functions are mixed together, and many functions, such as investigating, advocating, negotiating, testifying, rule-making an adjudicating, are carried out by the same agency. The reason for the breakdown of the separation-of-powers formula is not hard to find. It was felt by Congress, and state and municipal legislatures, that certain regulatory tasks could not be performed efficiently, rapidly, expertly, and with due concern for the public interest by the traditional branches of government. Accordingly, regulatory agencies were delegated powers to consider disputes from the earliest stage of investigation to the final stages of adjudication entirely within each agency itself, subject only to limited review in the regular courts.

11. The above passage states that the usual means for conflict resolution is through the use of 11.____
A. judicial trial B. administrative hearing
C. legislation D. regulatory agencies

12. The above passage *implies* that the use of administrative hearing in resolving conflict is a(n) _____ approach. 12.____
    A. traditional
    B. new
    C. dangerous
    D. experimental

13. The above passage states that the reason for the breakdown of the separation-of-powers formula in the administrative process is that 13.____
    A. Congress believed that certain regulatory tasks could be better performed by separate agencies
    B. legislative and executive functions are incompatible in the same agency
    C. investigative and regulatory functions are not normally reviewed by the courts
    D. state and municipal legislatures are more concerned with efficiency than with legality

14. An employee examining the summonses of individuals appearing for hearings noticed that the address on one summons was the same as that of an individual who had appeared earlier that day. He asked the second respondent if he knew the first respondent. 14.____
    The MOST appropriate evaluation of the employee's behavior is that he should
    A. not have mentioned any other respondent to the second respondent
    B. not waste time inspecting summonses in such detail
    C. be commended for inspecting summonses so carefully
    D. be commended for his investigation of the respondents

15. An employee is assigned to maintain all types of frequently used reference materials such as booklets and technical papers. He keeps these in a pile on a shelf in order of arrival. When new material arrives, he put it on top of the pile. Which of the following BEST evaluates the employee's handling of this reference material? 15.____
    His system is MOST likely to result in _____ filing and _____ retrieval.
    A. fast; slow
    B. slow; slow
    C. fast; fast
    D. slow; fast

16. An employee computes statistics relating to proceeding. The method he devised consists of organizing his source and summary documents in such a manner that at any time another employee can assume the work. This method takes a little more time than other possible methods. 16.____
    Which of the following statements BEST evaluates the judgment of the employee in devising such a method?
    The employee has used
    A. *good* judgment because it is important to provide for continuity
    B. *poor* judgment because he is not using the fastest method
    C. *good* judgment because, if a job is done as fast as possible, it becomes tiring
    D. *poor* judgment because it is not an employee's responsibility to prepare for a replacement

17. Assume that it is your job to receive incoming telephone calls. Those calls which you cannot handle yourself have to be transferred to the appropriate office. 17.____
If you receive an outside call for an extension line which is busy, the one of the following which you should do FIRST is to
   A. interrupt the person speaking on the extension and tell him a call is waiting
   B. tell the caller the line is busy and let him know every thirty seconds whether or not it is free
   C. leave the caller on *hold* until the extension is free
   D. tell the caller the line is busy and ask him if he wishes to wait

18. On one occasion in a certain office, an elderly employee collapsed, apparently the victim of a heart attack. Chaos broke out in the office as several people tried to help him and several others tried to get assistance. 18.____
Of the following, the MOST certain way of avoiding such chaos in the future is to
   A. keep a copy of heart attack procedures on file so that it can be referenced to by any member of the staff when an emergency occurs
   B. provide each member of the staff with a first aid book which is to be kept in an accessible location
   C. train all members of the staff in the proper procedure for handling such emergencies, assigning specific responsibilities
   D. post, in several places around the office, a list of specific procedures to follow in each of several different emergencies

19. Your superior has subscribed to several publications directly related to your divisions work, and he has asked you to see to it that the publications are circulated among the supervisory personnel in the division. There are eight supervisors involved. 19.____
The BEST method of insuring that all eight see these publications is to
   A. place the publication in the division's general reference library as soon as it arrives
   B. inform each supervisor whenever a publication arrives and remind all of them that they are responsible for reading it
   C. prepare a standard slip that can be stapled to each publication, listing the eight supervisors and saying, *Please read, initial your name, and pass along*
   D. send a memo to the eight supervisors saying that they may wish to purchase individual subscriptions in their own names if they are interested in seeing each issue

20. Assume that you have been asked to prepare a narrative summary of the monthly reports submitted by employees in your division. 20.____
In preparing your summary of this month's reports, the FIRST step to take is to
   A. read through the reports, noting their general content and any unusual features
   B. decide how many typewritten pages your summary should contain

C. make a written summary of each separate report, so that you will not have to go back to the original reports again
D. ask each employee which points he would prefer to see emphasized in your summary

21. Your superior has telephoned a number of key officials in your agency to ask whether they can meet at a certain time next month. He has found that they can all make it, and he has asked you to confirm the meeting. Which of the following is the BEST way to confirm such a meeting? 21.____
A. Note the meeting on your superior's calendar
B. Post a notice of the meeting on the agency bulletin board
C. Call the officials on the day of the meeting to remind them of the meeting
D. Write a memo to each official involved repeating the time and place of the meeting

22. Of the following, the worker who is MOST likely to create a problem in maintaining safety is one who 22.____
A. disregards hazards
B. feels tired
C. resents authority
D. gets bored

23. Assume that a new regulation requires that certain kinds of private organizations file information forms with your department. You have been asked to write the short explanatory message that will be printed on the front cover of the pamphlet containing the forms and instructions. Which of the following would be the MOST appropriate way of beginning this message? 23.____
A. Get the readers' attention by emphasizing immediately that there are legal penalties for organizations that fail to file before a certain date
B. Briefly state the nature of the enclosed forms and the types of organizations that must file
C. Say that your department is very sorry to have to put organizations to such an inconvenience
D. Quote the entire regulation adopted by the city, even if it is quite long and is expressed in complicated legal language

24. Suppose that you have been told to make up the vacation schedule for the 15 employees in a particular unit. In order for the unit to operate effectively, only a few employees can be on vacation at the same time. Which of the following is the MOST advisable approach in making up the schedule? 24.____
A. Draw up a schedule assigning vacations in alphabetical order
B. Find out when the supervisors want to take their vacations, and randomly assign whatever periods are left to the non-supervisory personnel
C. Assign the most desirable times to employees of longest standing, and the least desirable times to the newest employees
D. Have all employees state their own preferences, and then work out any conflicts in consultation with the people involved

25. Assume that you have been asked to prepare job descriptions for various positions in your department. 25.____
Which of the following are the BASIC points that should be covered in a job description?
   A. General duties and responsibilities of the position, with examples of day-to-day tasks
   B. Comments on the performances of present employees
   C. Estimates of the number of openings that may be available in each category during the coming year
   D. Instructions for carrying out the specific tasks assigned to your department

KEY (CORRECT ANSWERS)

1.	A	11.	A
2.	C	12.	B
3.	B	13.	A
4.	B	14.	A
5.	A	15.	A
6.	D	16.	A
7.	A	17.	D
8.	D	18.	C
9.	B	19.	C
10.	D	20.	A

21.	D
22.	A
23.	B
24.	D
25.	A

TEST 3

DIRECTIONS: Each question or incomplete statement is followed by several suggested answers or completions. Select the one that BEST answers the question or completes the statement. *PRINT THE LETTER OF THE CORRECT ANSWER IN THE SPACE AT THE RIGHT.*

Questions 1-6.

DIRECTIONS: Questions 1 through 6 consist of sets of names and addresses. In each question, the name and address in Column II should be an exact copy of the name and address in Column I. If there is:
a mistake only in the name, mark your answer A;
a mistake only in the address, mark your answer B;
a mistake in both name and address, mark your answer C;
NO mistake in either name or address, mark your answer D.

SAMPLE QUESTION

COLUMN I	COLUMN II
Christina Magnusson 288 Greene Street New York, NY 10003	Christina Magnusson 288 Greene Street New York, NY 10013

Since there is a mistake only in the address (the zone number should be 10003 instead of 10013), the answer to the sample question is B.

	COLUMN I	COLUMN II	
1.	Ms. Joan Kelly 313 Franklin Ave. Brooklyn, NY 11202	Ms. Joan Kielly 318 Franklin Ave. Brooklyn, NY 11202	1.____
2.	Mrs. Eileen Engel 47-24 86 Road Queens, NY 11122	Mrs. Ellen Engel 47-24 86 Road Queens, NY 11122	2.____
3.	Marcia Michaels 213 E. 81 St. New York, NY 10012	Marcia Michaels 213 E. 81 St. New York, NY 10012	3.____
4.	Rev. Edward J. Smyth 1401 Brandeis Street San Francisco, CA 96201	Rev. Edward J. Smyth 1401 Brandies Street San Francisco, CA 96201	4.____
5.	Alicia Rodriguez 24-68 81 St. Elmhurst, NY 11122	Alicia Rodriguez 2468 81 St. Elmhurst, NY 11122	5.____

	COLUMN I	COLUMN II	
6.	Ernest Eisemann 21 Columbia St. New York, NY 10007	Ernest Eisermann 21 Columbia St. New York, NY 10007	6.____

Questions 7-11.

DIRECTIONS: Questions 7 through 11 each consist of five serial numbers which must be arranged according to the directions given below.

The serial numbers of dollar bills in Column I begin and end with a capital letter and have an eight-digit number in between. They are to be arranged as follows:

First: In alphabetical order according to the first letter.
Second: When two or more serial numbers have the same first letter, in alphabetical order according to the last letter.
Third: When two or more serial numbers have the same first and last letters, in numerical order, beginning with the lowest number.

The serial numbers in Column I are numbered (1) through (5) in the order in which they are listed. In Column II, the numbers (1) through (5) are arranged in four different ways to show different arrangements of the corresponding serial numbers. Choose the answer in Column II in which the serial numbers are arranged according to the above rules.
SAMPLE QUESTION:

	COLUMN I		COLUMN II
(1)	E75044127B	(A)	4, 1, 3, 2, 5
(2)	B96399104A	(B)	4, 1 2, 3, 5
(3)	B93939086A	(C)	4, 3, 2 5, 1
(4)	B47064465H	(D)	3, 2, 5, 4, 1
(5)	B99040922A		

In the sample question, the four serial numbers starting with B should be put before the serial numbers starting with E. The serial numbers starting with B and ending with A should be put before the serial number starting with B and ending with H. The three serial numbers starting with B and ending with A should be listed in numerical order, beginning with the lowest number. The correct way to arrange the serial numbers, therefore, is

(3) B93939086A
(2) B96399104A
(5) B99040922A
(4) B47064465H
(1) B75044127B

Since the order of arrangement is 3, 2, 5, 4, 1, the answer to the sample question is (D).

	COLUMN I	COLUMN II	
7.	(1) S55126179E (2) R55136177Q (3) P55126177R (4) S55126178R (5) R55126180P	A. 1, 5, 2, 3, 4 B. 3, 4, 1, 5, 2 C. 3, 5, 2, 1, 4 D. 4, 3, 1, 5, 2	7.____
8.	(1) T64217813Q (2) I64217817O (3) T64218180 (4) I64217811Q (5) T64217816Q	A. 4, 1, 3, 2, 5 B. 2, 4, 3, 1, 5 C. 4, 1, 5, 2, 3 D. 2, 3, 4, 1, 5	8.____
9.	(1) C83261824G (2) C78361833C (3) G83261732G (4) C88261823C (5) G83261743C	A. 2, 4, 1, 5, 3 B. 4, 2, 1, 3, 5 C. 3, 1, 5, 2, 4 D. 2, 3, 5, 1, 4	9.____
10.	(1) A11710107H (2) H17110017A (3) A11170707A (4) II17170171H (5) A11710177A	A. 2, 1, 4, 3, 5 B. 3, 1, 5, 2, 4 C. 3, 4, 1, 5, 2 D. 3, 5, 1, 2, 4	10.____
11.	(1) R26794821S (2) O26794821T (3) M26794827Z (4) Q26794821R (5) S26794821P	A. 3, 2, 4, 1, 5 B. 3, 4, 2, 1, 5 C. 4, 2, 1, 3, 5 D. 5, 4, 1, 2, 3	11.____

Questions 12-16.

DIRECTIONS: Questions 12 through 16 each consist of three lines of code letters and numbers. The numbers on each line should correspond with the code letters on the same line in accordance with the table below.

Code Letters	Q	S	L	Y	M	O	U	N	W	Z
Corresponding Numbers	1	2	3	4	5	6	7	8	9	0

On some of the lines, an error exists in the coding. Compare the letters and numbers in each question carefully. If you find an error on:
only ONE of the lines in the question, mark your answer A;
any TWO lines in the question, mark your answer B;
all THREE lines in the question, mark your answer C;
NONE of the lines in the question, mark your answer D.

SAMPLE: MOQNWZQS – 56189012
QWNMOLYU – 19865347
LONLMYWN – 36835489

In the above sample, the first line is correct since each code letter, as listed, has the correct corresponding number. On the second line, an error exists because code letter M should have the letter number 5 instead of the number 6. On the third line, an error exists because the code letter W should have the number 9 instead of the number 8. Since there are errors on two of the three lines, the correct answer is B.

12.	SMUWOLQN	25796318	12.____
	ULSQNMZL	73218503	
	NMYQZUSL	85410723	
13.	YUWWMYQZ	47995410	13.____
	SOSOSQSO	26262126	
	ZUNLWMYW	07839549	
14.	QULSWZYN	17329045	14.____
	ZYLQWOYW	04319639	
	QLUYWZSO	13749026	
15.	NLQZOYUM	83106475	15.____
	SQMUWZOM	21579065	
	MMYWMZSQ	55498021	
16.	NQLOWZZU	81319007	16.____
	SMYLUNZO	25347806	
	UWMSNZOL	79528013	

Questions 17-24.

DIRECTIONS: Each of Questions 17 through 24 represents five cards to be filed, numbered 1 through 5 in Column I. Each card is made up of the employee's name, the date of a work assignment, and the work assignment code number shown in parentheses. The cards are to be filed according to the following rules.

First: File in alphabetical order.
Second: When two or more cards have the same employee's name, file according to the assignment date beginning with the earliest date.
Third: When to or more cards have the same employee's name and the same date, file according to the work assignment number beginning with the lowest number.

Column II shows the cards arranged in four different orders. Pick the answer (A, B, C, or D) in Column which shows the cards arranged correctly according to the above filing rules.

SAMPLE QUESTION

COLUMN I				COLUMN II
(1)	Cluney	4/8/19	(486503)	A. 2, 3, 4, 1, 5
(2)	Roster	5/10/18	(246611)	B. 2, 5, 1, 3, 4
(3)	Altool	10/15/18	(711433)	C. 3, 2, 1, 4, 5
(4)	Cluney	2/18/19	(527610)	D. 3, 5, 1, 4, 2
(5)	Cluney	4/8/19	(486500)	

The correct way to file the cards is:

(3)	Altool	10/15/18	(711433)
(5)	Cluney	4/8/19	(486500)
(1)	Cluney	4/8/19	(486503)
(4)	Cluney	12/18/19	(527610)
(2)	Roster	5/10/18	(246611)

The correct filing order is shown by the numbers in front of each name (3, 5, 1, 4, 2). The answer to the sample question is the letter in Column II in front of the numbers 3, 5, 1, 4, 2. This answer is D.

Now answer Questions 17 through 24 according to these rules.

	COLUMN I				COLUMN II	
17.	(1)	Kohls	4/2/19	(125677)	A. 1, 2, 3, 4, 5	17.____
	(2)	Keller	3/21/19	(129698)	B. 3, 2, 1, 4, 5	
	(3)	Jackson	4/10/19	(213541)	C. 3, 1, 2, 4, 5	
	(4)	Richards	1/9/20	(347236)	D. 5, 2, 1, 3, 4	
	(5)	Richmond	12/11/18	(379321)		
18.	(1)	Burroughs	5/27/19	(237896)	A. 1, 4, 3, 2, 5	18.____
	(2)	Charlson	1/16/19	(114537)	B. 4, 1, 5, 2, 2	
	(3)	Carlsen	12/2/19	(114377)	C. 1, 4, 3, 5, 2	
	(4)	Burton	5/1/19	(227096)	D. 4, 1, 3, 5, 2	
	(5)	Charlson	12/2/19	(114357)		
19.	(1)	Ungerer	11/11/19	(537924)	A. 1, 5, 3, 2, 4	19.____
	(2)	Winters	11/10/19	(657834)	B. 5, 1, 3, 4, 2	
	(3)	Ventura	12/1/19	(698694)	C. 3, 5, 1, 2, 4	
	(4)	Winters	10/11/18	(675654)	D. 1, 5, 3, 4, 2	
	(5)	Ungaro	11/10/19	(684325)		
20.	(1)	Norton	3/12/20	(071605)	A. 1, 4, 2, 3, 5	20.____
	(2)	Morris	2/26/20	(068931)	B. 3, 5, 2, 4, 1	
	(3)	Morse	5/12/20	(142358)	C. 2, 4, 3, 5, 1	
	(4)	Morris	2/26/20	(068391)	D. 4, 2, 5, 3, 1	
	(5)	Morse	2/26/20	(068391)		

21.	(1)	Eger	4/19/19	(874129)	A. 3, 4, 1, 2, 5	21.____
	(2)	Eihler	5/19/20	(875329)	B. 1, 4, 5, 2, 3	
	(3)	Ehrlich	11/19/19	(874839)	C. 4, 1, 3, 2, 5	
	(4)	Eger	4/19/19	(876129)	D. 1, 4, 3, 5, 2	
	(5)	Eihler	5/19/19	(874239)		
22.	(1)	Johnson	12/21/19	(786814	A. 2, 4, 3, 5, 1	22.____
	(2)	Johns	12/21/20	(801024)	B. 4, 2, 5, 3, 1	
	(3)	Johnson	12/12/20	(762814)	C. 4, 5, 3, 1, 2	
	(4)	Jackson	12/12/20	(862934)	D. 5, 3, 1, 2, 4	
	(5)	Johnson	12/12/20	(762184)		
23.	(1)	Fuller	7/12/19	(598310)	A. 2, 1, 5, 4, 3	23.____
	(2)	Fuller	7/2/19	(598301)	B. 1, 2, 4, 5, 3	
	(3)	Fuller	7/22/19	(598410)	C. 1, 4, 5, 2, 3	
	(4)	Fuller	7/17/20	(598710)	D. 2, 1, 3, 5, 3	
	(5)	Fuller	7/17/20	(598701)		
24.	(1)	Perrine	10/27/16	(637096)	A. 3, 4, 5, 1, 2	24.____
	(2)	Perrone	11/14/19	(767609)	B. 3, 2, 5, 4, 1	
	(3)	Perrault	10/15/15	(629706)	C. 5, 3, 1, 4, 2	
	(4)	Perrine	10/17/19	(373656)	D. 4, 5, 1, 2, 3	
	(5)	Perine	10/17/18	(376356)		

Questions 25-30.

DIRECTIONS: Questions 25 through 30 are to be answered on the basis of the information given in the following passage.

It is often said that no system will work if the people who carry it out do not want it to work. In too many cases, a departmental reorganization that seemed technically sound and economically practical has proved to be a failure because the planners neglected to take the human factor into account. The truth is that employees are likely to feel threatened when they learn that a major change is in the wind. It does not matter whether or not the change actually poses a threat to an employee; the fact that he believes it does or fears it might is enough to make him feel insecure. Among the dangers he fears, the foremost is the possibility that his job may cease to exist and that he may be laid off or shunted into a less skilled position at lower pay. Even if he knows that his own job category is secure, however, he is likely to fear losing some of the important intangible advantages of his present position for instance, he may fear that he will be separated from his present companions and thrust in with a group of strangers, or that he will find himself in a lower position on the organizational ladder if a new position is created above his.

It is important that management recognize these natural fears and take them into account in planning any kind of major change. While there is no cut-and-dried formula for preventing employee resistance, there are several steps that can be taken to reduce employees' fears and gain their cooperation. First, unwarranted fears can be dispelled if employees are kept informed of the planning from the start and if they know exactly what to expect. Next, assurance on matters such as retraining, transfers, and placement help should be given as soon as it is clear what direction the reorganization will take. Finally, employees' participation in the planning should be actively sought. There is a great psychological difference between feeling that a change is being forced upon one from the outside, and feeling that one is an insider who is helping to bring about a change.

25. According to the above passage, employees who are not in real danger of losing their jobs because of a proposed reorganization 25.____
    A. will be eager to assist in the reorganization
    B. will pay little attention to the reorganization
    C. should not be taken into account in planning the reorganization
    D. are nonetheless likely to feel threatened by the reorganization

26. The above passage mentions the *intangible advantages* of a position. Which of the following BEST describes the kind of advantages alluded to in the passage? 26.____
    A. Benefits such as paid holidays and vacations
    B. Satisfaction of human needs for things like friendship and status
    C. Qualities such as leadership and responsibility
    D. A work environment that meets satisfactory standards of health and safety

27. According to the above passage, an employee's fear that a reorganization may separate him from his present companions is a(n) 27.____
    A. childish and immature reaction to change
    B. unrealistic feeling, since this is not going to happen
    C. possible reaction that the planners should be aware of
    D. incentive to employees to participate in the planning

28. On the basis of the above passage, it would be *desirable*, when planning a departmental reorganization, to 28.____
    A. be governed by employee feelings and attitudes
    B. give some employees lower positions
    C. keep employees informed
    D. lay off those who are less skilled

29. What does the above passage say can be done to help gain employees' cooperation in a reorganization? 29.____
    A. Making sure that the change is technically sound, that it is economically practical, and that the human factor is taken into account
    B. Keeping employees fully informed, offering help in fitting them into new positions, and seeking their participation in the planning
    C. Assuring employees that they will not be laid off, that they will not be reassigned to a group of strangers, and that no new positions will be created on the organization ladder
    D. Reducing employees' fears, arranging a retraining program, and providing for transfers

30. Which of the following suggested title would be MOST appropriate for this passage? 30.____
   A. Planning a Departmental Reorganization
   B. Why Employees are Afraid
   C. Looking Ahead to the Future
   D. Planning for Change: The Human Factor

KEY (CORRECT ANSWERS)

1.	C	11.	A	21.	D
2.	A	12.	D	22.	B
3.	D	13.	D	23.	D
4.	B	14.	B	24.	C
5.	C	15.	A	25.	D
6.	A	16.	C	26.	B
7.	C	17.	B	27.	C
8.	B	18.	A	28.	C
9.	A	19.	B	29.	B
10.	D	20.	D	30.	D

EXAMINATION SECTION
TEST 1

DIRECTIONS: Each question or incomplete statement is followed by several suggested answers or completions. Select the one that BEST answers the question or completes the statement. *PRINT THE LETTER OF THE CORRECT ANSWER IN THE SPACE AT THE RIGHT.*

1. An efficient telephone operator is one who 1.____

   A. is always busy
   B. is well-educated
   C. has had years of experience
   D. performs her duties with speed and accuracy

2. A PBX operator in a city department should always be courteous to the public because 2.____

   A. she will win many new personal friends that way
   B. courteous attention will encourage people to use the telephone more often
   C. courtesy on the telephone creates good will toward the employer
   D. the caller is spending money to make the call and is, therefore, entitled to courtesy

3. A newly-appointed telephone operator should try to learn about the organization and operation of her department so that she may 3.____

   A. foresee all emergencies
   B. avoid antagonizing her superiors
   C. justify mistakes
   D. perform her duties properly

4. Assume that the switchboard operator in your department also serves as the receptionist. A man requesting information speaks to you in an abrupt manner. 4.____
   You should

   A. turn away from him and continue with your work without answering him
   B. disregard his manner and give him the desired information
   C. give him the information he requests, but in a similar manner
   D. tell him he will have to speak more politely before you can answer him

5. In opening and sorting the mail coming into an office, envelopes should not be discarded until after the letter has been examined because 5.____

   A. the person to whom the letter should be forwarded cannot usually be determined without the envelope
   B. letter writers often forget to include a return address in their letters
   C. envelopes often have interesting and valuable new stamps on them
   D. the subject of the letter is not always clearly stated on the envelope

6. In most city departments, employees in the same office select their vacation periods in the order of seniority. The MOST probable reason for using this method is to 6.____

   A. reward employees with the longest service

B. give every employee the time he desires
C. avoid overlapping vacation schedules
D. give new employees preference as to their vacation time

7. Telephone operators should not engage in long personal calls while on duty MAINLY because 7.___

A. such calls raise the city's telephone bill and may ultimately cause a rise in the city's tax rate
B. most personal phone calls are unnecessary
C. such calls annoy the supervisor and often cause personal attention
D. personal calls interfere with efficient operation at the switchboard

8. The one of the following forms of records which is LEAST essential for a PBX operator in a city department is a 8.___

A. list of all elected officials of the state with their office addresses
B. directory of employees and their extension numbers
C. list of all city departments and their telephone numbers
D. list of the extensions and trunks used for night connections

9. While on duty at the switchboard, you receive an incoming call for Miss Jones, who has recently resigned. 9.___
You should

A. tell the caller, *Miss Jones is no longer in this office,* and disconnect the call
B. ask the caller whether someone else may help him as Miss Jones has resigned
C. tell the caller employees are not allowed to receive personal calls in the office
D. tell the caller that Miss Jones may be reached at her home address

10. If you were asked to prepare a list of out-of-town calls and telegrams for the chief clerk's office on the basis of your daily records, the BEST way to check your list for absolute accuracy would be to 10.___

A. prepare a second copy of the list and check the two copies
B. ask another operator to read the copy aloud while you check against the original records
C. check the one or two points in the list where errors are most likely to be made
D. examine the list to see whether all entries look reasonable

11. In offices where the volume of telephone calls is large and requires the full attention of the operator, the switchboard is usually set up in a separate room away from the public. 11.___
The MOST probable reason for doing this is that it

A. is the only space available for the switchboard
B. gives the telephone operators privacy so that they can relax without embarrassment
C. prevents the public from overhearing confidential calls
D. permits the operators to work without interruptions or disturbing sounds

12. Of the following, the LEAST valid reason for keeping tallies of incoming calls is to determine 12.____

    A. the volume of work which the operator is required to handle
    B. whether the equipment is adequate to handle the volume of incoming calls
    C. the distribution of calls among the various bureaus in the department
    D. whether there are any improper charges in the telephone bill on collect calls

13. Of the following, the number which should be pronounced as indicated is: 13.____

    A. Three, one, nine, thirty-four hundred
    B. Two, six, seven, forty-two, thirty
    C. Nine, six, two, five, oh, four, one
    D. Five, six, four, three, oh, oh, oh

14. When a name given over the telephone is apt to be misunderstood, it is BEST to 14.____

    A. repeat the name again and again until the other person says he understands what you are saying
    B. spell the name out rapidly and pronounce it once again
    C. spell the name out slowly, using proper names to identify each letter
    D. explain that this is a very difficult name to pronounce and ask the other person to listen closely as you pronounce the name slowly and distinctly

15. In even year elections, voters will ALWAYS elect 15.____

    A. members of the House of Representatives
    B. the Governor and other state officials
    C. local officials only
    D. both Senators from their state

16. The one of the following who is NOT appointed is the 16.____

    A. Police Commissioner
    B. President of the United States
    C. Commissioner of Investigation
    D. Chief Magistrate

17. Members of the House of Representatives are elected by 17.____

    A. majority vote of the residents of each congressional district
    B. proportional representation on a county-wide basis, according to the number of votes case in each county
    C. city-wide vote, according to the number of residents in each borough
    D. the county committees of each of the major political parties

18. Congress may NOT enact laws to 18.____

    A. provide funds for large-scale public housing to ease the present shortage
    B. reduce income taxes for low-income families
    C. restrict the activities of labor unions
    D. make direct grants to parochial schools

19. In a given city department, where a record was kept of all calls, the number of incoming calls during a given week were: 2,070 on Monday, 1,963 on Tuesday, 1,826 on Wednesday, 2,153 on Thursday, 2,019 on Friday, and 987 on Saturday. The total number of incoming calls for the week is 19.____

A. 11,018 B. 10,918 C. 10,131 D. 11,118

20. In another department, the number of outgoing calls during the week was 205 on Monday, 241 on Tuesday, 248 on wednesday, 274 on Thursday, and 187 on Friday. The average number of outgoing calls for the week is 20.____

A. 241 B. 231 C. 211 D. 203

21. The telephone user should try to speak 21.____

A. in an expressionless and impersonal manner
B. at a rate of 350 words per minute as telephone time is valuable
C. with as little facial expression as possible as she cannot be seen anyway
D. distinctly, especially when pronouncing numbers

22. A flashing cord signal indicates to the operator that the extension user requires 22.____

A. disconnecting
B. a line
C. service
D. a number

23. The CHIEF difference between a PBX and a Monitor Board is that a Monitor Board 23.____

A. requires more operators
B. cannot adequately handle as many incoming and outgoing calls
C. is more expensive to install
D. requires longer training to operate correctly

24. Of the following, cut-offs are MOST frequently caused by failure to trace 24.____

A. jacks B. cords C. plugs D. signals

25. When ringing on an extension call, it is BEST to ring for about 25.____

A. two seconds, with a ten second pause followed by another two second ring
B. thirty seconds, continuously
C. fifteen seconds, with a fifteen second pause followed by another fifteen second ring
D. ten seconds, with a two second pause followed by another ten second ring

26. Assuming that the following signals appear simultaneously, the one which should be given FIRST attention is a(n) ______ signal. 26.____

A. flashing
B. inside extension
C. incoming trunk
D. disconnect

27. The efficient PBX operator USUALLY employs plugs from left to right in order to 27.____

A. prevent *busy* signals
B. save time
C. give all plugs equal wear
D. insure clear transmission

28. If several extension signals are lighted, the operator should answer them by giving priority to 28.____

A. outgoing calls
B. lower extension numbers
C. signals which are nearer to the operator
D. signals which appeared first

29. The proper procedure to follow if a called party answers before the operator disconnects from his line on a cancelled call is for the operator to 29.____

A. ask the called party to excuse the call
B. disconnect the front cord
C. ring the called extension again
D. give a *don't answer* report

30. The LEAST satisfactory answer when reporting a busy extension to an outside caller is: 30.____

A. Mr. Smith's extension is busy. Will you talk with anyone else?
B. Mr. Smith's extension is busy. Will you call again tomorrow when he will be less busy?
C. Mr. Smith's extension is busy. Will you wait?
D. If you will leave your name and number, I will tell Mr. Smith you called

31. Signals on incoming trunk calls should not be plugged out unless the operator is ready to establish the desired connection immediately because 31.____

A. additional calls cannot come in on a line that is plugged out
B. the caller may abandon his call when the ringing signal stops if he does not get prompt service
C. the board looks more cheerful when many signals are lighted at once
D. slow answers create an impression of a busy office upon the caller

32. Progress reports are made CHIEFLY 32.____

A. because they are required by the telephone company
B. in order to have a record of the number of calls made in a given period of time
C. to test the efficiency of the operator
D. to assure the caller that the operator has not forgotten him

33. A tie line connects a PBX board with 33.____

A. a front cord
B. the supervisor
C. another PBX system
D. the central office operator

34. Mechanical faults such as dim signals should be reported by the PBX operator to the 34.____

A. office clerk in charge of supplies and equipment
B. central office operator
C. nearest business office manager
D. repair service

35. Switchboard service is considered to be efficient when the time between the appearance of an incoming call signal on the board and the time that the operator acknowledges the call is not more than ______ seconds. 35.___

A. 5
B. 8
C. 10
D. 7

36. If conversation on an extension-to-extension connection is indistinct, the PBX operator should FIRST 36.___

A. use a different pair of cords to complete the connection
B. ask one of the extension users to use a different extension
C. request a new PBX board
D. ask the two parties to speak louder

37. The term *overlapping operation* can MOST appropriately be used to describe the work of the PBX operator when 37.___

A. two operators at a multiple-position board insert plugs into the same jack
B. an operator at a two-position board inserts her plug into a jack at the adjoining board
C. the operator attends to two operations in the same movement
D. several cords extend over a number of jacks on the same level of the switchboard

38. When making a progress report, the operator should take special care to operate the proper 38.___

A. plug
B. buzzer key
C. jack
D. talking key

39. In transferring an incoming call, the PBX operator should make sure that the front key is in talking position in order to avoid 39.___

A. a cut-off
B. dial tone
C. overlapping
D. a recall signal

40. For the telephone operator to keep the listening key open while an extension user is carrying on a conversation with an outside call is 40.___

A. *good,* because it is possible for her to take down the connection immediately after the conversation ends and thus speed up service
B. *bad,* because it slows down her work when her attention should be focused on the board
C. *good,* because it helps to keep the operator informed as to what is going on in the office
D. *bad,* because she might be tempted to join in the conversation and thus annoy the callers

41. The LEAST accurate of the following statements is: 41.___

A. The battery key should be in the *on* position when the board is in operation
B. Handling the cords by the hard rubber shell of the plug will prevent breaking of wires in the cords
C. For the best service, the PBX operator should speak in a loud voice, holding the mouthpiece two inches from her lips
D. When transferring a call, the front key should be operated to the talking position until the cord is inserted into the jack of the desired extension

42. The LEAST accurate of the following statements is: 42.____

A. Both cords should be disconnected whenever both supervisory signals appear
B. The line from the telephone switchboard to the central office is known as a trunk line
C. The back cord (the one farthest from the operator) should be used to answer an extension call
D. It is absolutely essential that all disconnecting is completed before incoming trunk signals are answered

43. The LEAST accurate of the following statements is: 43.____

A. An extension user should hold the line for the completion of local and toll calls
B. The PBX operator should chat frequently with extension users as a means of keeping their good will
C. The transmission of a message is reduced materially if the operator listens in
D. Prompt answering by extension users is helpful to the PBX operator as well as good office manners

44. The LEAST accurate of the following statements is: 44.____

A. Cords on which the supervisory signals are dim should be used on extension-to-extension calls so that the others will be available for incoming calls
B. Third party connections are caused by operating more than one listening key at a time
C. The operator should check to see whether any of the night connections are in use before disconnecting them in the morning
D. Either the firm name or the telephone number should be announced in answering incoming calls

45. The MOST accurate of the following statements is: 45.____

A. If the PBX operator should find a discrepancy between her records and the telephone bill, she should correct her record to agree with the bill and be more careful in the future
B. The PBX operator rings an outgoing call by pulling the appropriate front key
C. When the PBX operator wishes to have time or charges quoted, she should ask long distance for this information when she places the call
D. The ringing key should be pulled toward the operator before plugging into an extension jack

46. The MOST accurate of the following statements is: 46.____

A. If there are any non-consecutive trunk lines on the board, the operator should reserve them for incoming calls
B. To ring on an extension, the ringing key should be pushed toward the switchboard
C. When the signal light associated with an extension jack is on, it indicates that the receiver is off the extension
D. When an extension user is dialing, the operator should cut in if the supervisory signal flickers rapidly

47. The MOST accurate of the following statements is: 47.____

A. In a rush period, the operator should plug into the jacks as the signals occur and then answer them as soon as she can
B. A caller on an incoming trunk line will be cut off if he tries to flash the operator in order to have his call transferred to another extension
C. Charges for long distance telephone calls start when the number is given to the central office operator
D. A PBX operator should be more careful in her choice of words when speaking to a superior than when giving information over the telephone

48. The LEAST accurate of the following statements is: 48.____

A. In answering an incoming long distance collect call for one of the extension users, the PBX operator should accept the call and bill the caller for the amount of the charge
B. Key sleeves help to distinguish between disconnects on completed calls and connections which have not yet been established and, therefore, require progress reports
C. Time is saved in making long distance calls if the caller knows the number
D. The operator should select the highest numbered idle trunk for outgoing calls

49. The MOST accurate of the following statements is: 49.____

A. Any two plugs may be used to complete a connection
B. *Reversing the charges* for a long distance call means that the person initiating the call pays for the charge
C. On a two-position board, the operator should answer signals on the next position as well as on her own position
D. An operator should answer extension signals in preference to incoming trunk signals

50. The MOST accurate of the following statements is: 50.____

A. When night connections have been established, one extension user can call any other extension
B. In removing the connecting cords from the jacks, the trunk line should be released first
C. In case of an emergency such as fire, if the PBX operator does not have the desired telephone number at hand, she should call Information and say, *I want to report a fire*
D. In a multiple switchboard, the jack should be tested on all incoming and inside calls to see if it is busy

51. The LEAST accurate of the following statements is: 51.____

A. If an extension user on an established connection moves the receiver hook slowly up and down several times, a supervisory signal will flash
B. An extension user cannot dial his call unless the back key is operated toward the switchboard
C. It is good telephone practice to pronounce the number *nine* as *ni-en* in order to avoid misunderstanding

D. The operator need not bother to keep a list of frequently called numbers as Information can supply them when needed

52. The LEAST accurate of the following statements is: 52.____

A. Calls to the business office of the telephone company may be made without any charge
B. If the operator is right-handed, she should use the cords on the right side of the board as much as possible
C. In setting up night connections, the back keys should be operated to the through dialing position
D. When signalling a central office operator on an existing trunk connection, the front key should be in talking position

53. The MOST accurate of the following statements is: 53.____

A. Only one hand should be used in operating a switchboard
B. In taking down a connection, the extension cord should be released first
C. When answering an extension signal, it is not necessary to acknowledge the extension user's order
D. Incoming calls should be answered with a phrase such as, *Extension number, please*

54. The LEAST accurate of the following statements is: 54.____

A. If a called extension is busy and the calling party asks to be called back, the operator should make a written record of the request
B. The operator should acknowledge an order so that the calling party will know that the order is understood
C. To flash the central office operator on an existing connection, the back key should be moved all the way back and held until central office answers
D. To ring an extension, the ringing key is pulled toward the operator

55. The MOST accurate of the following statements is: 55.____

A. The conversation will be less distinct if the listening key is left open after the connection is made
B. When traffic becomes heavy, the buzzer key should be operated to the *on* position
C. The PBX operator should request that a call be made collect after the call is completed
D. When setting up night connections, the battery key should be operated to the *off* position before the night keys are operated

Questions 56-70.

DIRECTIONS: Questions 56 through 70 consist of groups of four words each. These are divided into syllables, one of which is underlined in each word to indicate the syllable that is stressed in pronouncing the word. In three of the four words in each item, the correct syllable is underlined; in the other word, the syllable which is underlined, if stressed, would give an incorrect pronunciation. For each item, indicate which of the four words lettered A, B, C, or D would be INCORRECTLY pronounced if the underlined syllable is stressed.

56. A. graph-i-cal B. gov-ern-men-tal 56.____
C. guar-an-tee D. guard-i-an-ship

57. A. el-e-va-tor B. en-tire 57.____
C. ex-qui-site D. ev-i-dent-ly

58. A. sub-jec-tive B. sub-li-mate 58.____
C. sub-trac-tion D. sub-sti-tute

59. A. pre-lim-i-nar-y B. pre-lude 59.____
C. pos-i-tive-ly D. pref-er-a-ble

60. A. cir-cu-late B. cir-cum-stan-tial 60.____
C. ci-vil-i-ty D. cig-a-rette

61. A. dy -nam-ic B. du-pli-cate 61.____
A. du-ra-tion B. de-fin-i-tive

62. A. ad-min-i-ster B. ad-mit-tance 62.____
C. ad-vo-cate D. a-gen-cy

63. A. ap-pel-late B. au-thor-i-ty 63.____
C. at-tend-ant D. at-ti-tude

64. A. fal-si-fy B. fed-er-a-tion 64.____
C. fil-i-bus-ter D. fi-nal-ly

65. A. mon-e-tary B. mu-nif-i-cent 65.____
C. mo-nop-o-ly D. mor-al-ism

66. A. na-tion-al-ly B. nat-u-ral-ism 66.____
C. ne-ces-si-ty D. neu-tral-i-ty

67. A. sac-ri-fice B. se-cu-ri-ty 67.____
C. se-lec-tive D. suc-ces-sion

68. A. stand-ard-ize B. sta-tion-ar-y 68.____
C. sta-tis-tics D. sup-ple-ment

69. A. ju-rid-i-cal B. ju-ris-dic-tion 69.____
C. jus-tiOfi-ca-tion D. ju-di-ci-ar-y

70. A. le-git-i-mate B. leg-is-la-tion 70.____
C. leg-is-la-tor D. leg-ibl-y

Questions 71-80.

DIRECTIONS: Questions 71 through 80 consist of sentences which may or may not contain errors in grammar, punctuation, or spelling. Examine each sentence carefully. Then write your answer in the space at the right corresponding to the number of the sentence. If the sentence is CORRECT, write A as your answer. If the sentence contains an error in grammar, write B as your answer; if an error in punctuation, write C; and if an error in spelling, write D. All incorrect sentences contain but one error, either B, C, or D. Do not write more than one letter for any sentence.

71. The supervisor asked who would be willing to work late that night? 71._____

72. Good appearance is an asset in business as well as in personal relations. 72._____

73. Work with a student organization teaches one to cooperate with others, to take responsibility, and to direct others. 73._____

74. The most confusing part about a switchboard are the many flashing signals. 74._____

75. Two letters arrived today but, no one answered them. 75._____

76. Complaints against telephone operators who are efficient are comparitively few. 76._____

77. The supervisor should designate who will do the work in an emergency. 77._____

78. The safeguards that are taken to insure an accurate record of calls are in the interest of the telephone user as well as the company. 78._____

79. The court did not decide the question of whom was to be appointed guardian. 79._____

80. Employees who perform satisfactorily on the job receive adequate reconition in their service rating reports. 80._____

KEY (CORRECT ANSWERS)

1.	D	21.	D	41.	C	61.	A
2.	C	22.	C	42.	D	62.	C
3.	D	23.	B	43.	B	63.	B
4.	B	24.	B	44.	A	64.	C
5.	B	25.	A	45.	C	65.	B
6.	A	26.	A	46.	C	66.	D
7.	D	27.	C	47.	B	67.	D
8.	A	28.	D	48.	A	68.	D
9.	C	29.	A	49.	C	69.	C
10.	B	30.	B	50.	D	70.	B
11.	D	31.	B	51.	D	71.	C
12.	D	32.	D	52.	B	72.	D
13.	C	33.	C	53.	B	73.	A
14.	C	34.	D	54.	C	74.	B
15.	A	35.	C	55.	A	75.	C
16.	B	36.	A	56.	B	76.	D
17.	A	37.	C	57.	C	77.	A
18.	D	38.	D	58.	A	78.	A
19.	A	39.	A	59.	C	79.	B
20.	B	40.	B	60.	D	80.	D

EXAMINATION SECTION

TEST 1

DIRECTIONS: Each question or incomplete statement is followed by several suggested answers or completions. Select the one that BEST answers the question or completes the statement. *PRINT THE LETTER OF THE CORRECT ANSWER IN THE SPACE AT THE RIGHT.*

1. Public organizations usually share each of the following customer-service problems with private organizations EXCEPT 1.____
   A. aversion to risk B. staff-heaviness
   C. provision of reverse incentives D. control-apportionment functions

2. A service representative demonstrates interpersonal skills by 2.____
   A. identifying a customer's expectations
   B. learning how to use a new office telephone system
   C. studying a competitor's approach to service
   D. anticipating how a customer will react to certain situations

3. Of the following, _____ is NOT generally considered to be a common reason for flaws in an organization's customer focus. 3.____
   A. commissioned employee compensation
   B. full problem-solving authority for front-line personnel
   C. inadequate hiring practices
   D. specific, case-oriented policy and procedural statements

4. According to MOST research, approximately _____ of dissatisfied customers will actually complain or make their dissatisfaction with a product known to the organization. 4.____
   A. 5% B. 25% C. 50% D. 75%

5. Which of the following is an example of an expected benefit associated with a product or service? 5.____
   A. Before buying a car, a customer believes she will not have to take the car in for repairs every few months.
   B. A customer in a sporting goods store tells a salesperson exactly what kind of trolling motor will meet the requirements of the lakes the customer wanted to fish.
   C. A supermarket shopper buys a loaf of bread, believing that the bread will remain fresh for a few days.
   D. An airline passenger discover that the meals served on board are good.

6. During a meeting with a service representative, a customer makes an apparently reasonable request. However, the representative knows that satisfying the customer's request will violate a rule that is part of the organization's policy. Although the representative feels that an exception to the rule should be made in this case, she is not sure whether an exception can or should be made. 6.____

The BEST course of action for the representative would be to
- A. deny the request and apologize, explaining the company policy
- B. rely on good judgment and allow the request
- C. try to steer the customer toward a similar but clearly permissible request
- D. contact a manager or more experienced peer to handle the request

7. While organizing an effective customer service department, it would be LEAST effective to 7.____
   - A. create procedures for relaying reasons for complaints to other departments
   - B. set up a clear chain-of-command for handling specific customer complaints
   - C. continually monitor performance of front-line personnel
   - D. give front-line people full authority to resolve all customer dissatisfaction

8. Of the following, _____ is an example of *tangible* service. 8.____
   - A. an interior decorator telling his/her ideas to a potential client
   - B. a salesclerk giving a written cost estimate to a potential buyer
   - C. an automobile salesman telling a showroom customer about a car's performance
   - D. a stockbroker offering investment advice over the telephone

9. As a rule, a customer service representative who handles telephones should always answer a call within no more than _____ ring(s). 9.____
   A. 1 B. 3 C. 5 D. 8

10. In order to be as useful as possible to an organization, feedback received from customers should NOT be 10.____
    - A. portrayed on a line graph or similar device
    - B. used to provide a general overview
    - C. focused on end-use customers
    - D. available upon demand

11. Of all the customers who switch to competing organizations approximately _____ percent do so because of poor service. 11.____
    A. 25 B. 40 C. 75 D. 95

12. When customers offer information that is incorrect in their complaints, a service representative should do each of the following EXCEPT 12.____
    - A. assume that the customer is making an innocent mistake
    - B. look for opportunities to educate the customer
    - C. calmly state a reasonable argument that will correct the customer's mistake
    - D. believe the customer until he/she is able to find proof of his/her error

13. In order to insure that a customer feels comfortable in a face-to-face meeting, a service representative should 13.____
    A. avoid discussing controversial issues
    B. use personal terms such as *dear* or *friend*
    C. address the customer by his/her first name
    D. tell a few jokes

14. Customer satisfaction is MOST effectively measured in terms of 14.____
    A. cost B. benefit C. convenience D. value

15. Making a sale is NOT considered good service when 15.____
    A. there are no alternatives to the subject of the customer's complaint
    B. when the original product or service is outdated
    C. an add-in feature will forestall other problems
    D. the product or service the customer has been using is the wrong product

16. When dealing with an indecisive customer, the service representative should 16.____
    A. expand available possibilities
    B. offer a way out of unsatisfying decisions
    C. ask probing questions for understanding
    D. steer the customer toward one particular decision

17. Of the following, _____ would NOT be a source of direct organizational service promises. 17.____
    A. advertising materials
    B. published organizational policies
    C. contracts
    D. the customer's past experience with the organization

18. Generally, the only kind of organization that can validly circumvent the requirements of customer service is one that 18.____
    A. cannot afford to staff an entire service department
    B. relies solely on the sale of ten or fewer items per year
    C. has little or no competition
    D. serves clients that are separated from consumers

19. When using the problem-solving approach to solve the problem of an upset customer, the service representative should FIRST 19.____
    A. express respect for the customer
    B. identify the customer's expectations
    C. outline a solution or alternatives
    D. listen to understand the problem

20. During face-to-face meetings with strangers such as service personnel, most North Americans consider a comfortable proximity to be 20.____
    A. 6 inches - 1 foot B. 8 inches - 1½ feet
    C. 1½ - 2 feet D. 2-4 feet

21. When answering phone calls, a service representative should ALWAYS do each of the following EXCEPT 21.____
    A. state his/her name
    B. give the name of the organization or department
    C. ask probing questions
    D. offer assistance

22. If a customer appears to be emotionally neutral when lodging a complaint, it would be MOST appropriate for a service representative to demonstrate ____ in reaction to the complaint. 22.____
    A. urgency B. empathy C. nonchalance D. surprise

23. When soliciting customer feedback, standard practice is to limit the number of questions asked to APPROXIMATELY 23.____
    A. 3-5 B. 5-10 C. 10-20 D. 15-40

24. A customer has purchased an item from a company and has been told that the item will be delivered in two weeks. However, a customer service representative later discovers that deliveries are running about three days behind schedule. 24.____
    The MOST appropriate course of action for the representative would be to
    A. call the customer immediately, apologize for the delay, and await the customer's response
    B. call the customer a few days before delivery is due and explain that the delay is the fault of the delivery company
    C. immediately sent out a *loaner* of the ordered item to the customer
    D. wait for the customer to note the delay and contact the organization

25. Most research show that _____% of what is communicated between people during face-to-face meetings is conveyed through words alone. 25.____
    A. 10 B. 30 C. 50 D. 80

KEY (CORRECT ANSWERS)

1. D
2. D
3. B
4. A
5. B

6. D
7. B
8. B
9. B
10. B

11. B
12. C
13. A
14. D
15. A

16. B
17. D
18. C
19. A
20. C

21. C
22. D
23. B
24. A
25. A

TEST 2

DIRECTIONS: Each question or incomplete statement is followed by several suggested answers or completions. Select the one that BEST answers the question or completes the statement. *PRINT THE LETTER OF THE CORRECT ANSWER IN THE SPACE AT THE RIGHT.*

1. When working cooperatively to identify specific internal service targets, personnel typically encounter each of the following obstacles EXCEPT 1.____
   A. rapidly-changing work environment
   B. philosophical differences about the nature of service
   C. specialized knowledge of certain personnel exceeds that of others
   D. a chain-of-command that isolates the end user

2. Which of the following is an example of an external customer relationship? 2.____
   A. Baggage clerks to travelers
   B. Catering staff to flight attendants
   C. Managers to ticketing agents
   D. Maintenance workers to ground crew

3. When a service representative puts a customer's complaint in writing, results will be produced more quickly than if the representative had merely told someone. 3.____
   Which of the following is NOT generally considered to be a reason for this?
   A. The complaint can be more easily routed to parties capable of solving the problem.
   B. Management will understand the problem more clearly.
   C. The representative can more clearly see the main aspects of the complaint.
   D. The complaint and response will become a part of a public record.

4. A customer service representative creates a client file, which contains notes about what particular clients want, need, and expect. 4.____
   Which of the following basic areas of learning is the representative exercising?
   A. Interpersonal skills
   B. Product and service knowledge
   C. Customer knowledge
   D. Technical skills

5. A customer complains that a desired product, which is currently on sale, is needed in at least two weeks, but the company is out of stock and the product will not be available for another four weeks. 5.____
   Of the following, the BEST example of a service *recovery* on the part of a representative would be to
   A. apologize for the company's inability to serve the customer while expressing a wish to deal with the customer in the future
   B. attempt to steer the customer's interest toward an unrelated product
   C. offer a comparable model at the same sale price

6. Of the following, _____ is NOT generally considered to be a function of closed questioning when dealing with a customer. 6.____
   A. understanding requests
   B. getting the customer to agree
   C. clarifying what has been said
   D. summarizing a conversation

7. When dealing with a customer who speaks with a heavy foreign accent, a service representative should NOT 7.____
   A. speak loudly
   B. speak slowly
   C. avoid humor or witticism
   D. repeat what has been said

8. If a customer service representative is aware that time will be a factor in the delivery of service to a customer, the representative should FIRST 8.____
   A. warn the customer that the organization is under time constraints
   B. suggest that the customer return another time
   C. ask the customer to suggest a service deadline
   D. tell the customer when service can reasonably be expected

9. In relation to a customer service representative's view of an organization, the customer's view of the company tends to be 9.____
   A. more negative
   B. more objective
   C. broader in scope
   D. less forgiving

10. When asked to define the factors that determine whether they will do business with an organization, most customers maintain that _____ is the MOST important. 10.____
    A. friendly employees
    B. having their needs met
    C. convenience
    D. product pricing

11. While a customer is stating her service requirements, a service representative should do each of the following EXCEPT 11.____
    A. ask questions about complex or unclear information
    B. formulate a response to the customer's remarks
    C. repeat critical information
    D. attempt to roughly outline the customer's main points

12. If a customer service representative must deal with other member of a service team in order to resolve a problem, the representative should avoid 12.____
    A. conveying every single detail of a problem to others
    B. suggesting deadlines for problem resolution
    C. offering opinions about the source of the problem
    D. explaining the specifics concerning the need for resolution

13. Of the following, the LAST step in the resolution of a service problem should be 13.____
    A. the offer of an apology for the problem
    B. asking probing questions to understand and conform the nature of the problem
    C. listening to the customer's description of the problem
    D. determining and implementing a solution to the problem

14. _____ is a poor scheduling strategy for a customer service representative. 14.____
   A. Performing the easiest tasks first
   B. Varying work routines
   C. Setting deadlines that will allow some restful work periods
   D. Doing similar jobs at the same time

15. The MOST defensible reason for the avoidance of customer satisfaction guarantees is 15.____
   A. buyer remorse
   B. repeated customer contact
   C. high costs
   D. ability of buyers to take advantage of guarantees

16. A customer service representative demonstrates knowledge and courtesy to customers and is able to convey trust, competence, and confidence. 16.____
Of the following service factors, the representative is demonstrating
   A. assurance
   B. responsiveness
   C. empathy
   D. reliability

17. If a service representative is involved in sales, _____ is NOT one of the primary pieces of information he/she will need to supply the customer. 17.____
   A. cost of product or service
   B. how the product works
   C. how to repair the product
   D. available payment plans

18. A customer appears to be experiencing extreme feelings of anger and frustration when loading a complaint. 18.____
The MOST appropriate reaction for a service representative to demonstrate is
   A. urgency
   B. empathy
   C. nonchalance
   D. surprise

19. Of the following obstacles to customer service, _____ is NOT generally considered to be unique to public organizations. 19.____
   A. ambivalence toward clients
   B. limited competition
   C. a rule-based mission
   D. clients who are not really customers

20. Most customers report that the MOST frustrating aspect of waiting in line for service is 20.____
   A. not knowing how long they will have to wait for service
   B. rudeness on the part of the service representatives
   C. being expected to wait for service at all
   D. unfair prioritizing on the part of service representatives

21. Which of the following is an example of an *assumed benefit* associated with a product or service? 21.____
A customer
   A buys a sporty sedan and finds that its tight turning ratio makes it easy to park
   B. visits a fast-food restaurant because she is in a hurry to get dinner over with

C. buys a videotape and believes it will not cause damage to her VCR
D. tells a salesman that he wants to purchase a high-status automobile

22. On an average, for every complaint received by an organization, there are actually about _____ customers who have legitimate problems. 22.____
A. 3 B. 5 C. 15 D. 25

23. Once a customer problem is identified, each of the following should become a part of the service recovery process EXCEPT 23.____
A. apologizing
B. an offer of compensation
C. empathetic listening
D. sympathy

24. As a rule, customers who telephone organizations should not be put on hold for any longer than 24.____
A. 10 seconds
B. 60 seconds
C. 5 minutes
D. 10 minutes

25. The LEAST effective way to make customers feel as if they are a part of a service team would be to ask them for 25.____
A. information about similar products/services they have used
B. opinions about how to solve problems
C. personally contact the department that can best help them
D. opinions about particular products and services

KEY (CORRECT ANSWERS)

1. B
2. A
3. D
4. C
5. D

6. A
7. A
8. C
9. C
10. B

11. B
12. C
13. A
14. A
15. B

16. A
17. C
18. B
19. B
20. A

21. C
22. D
23. D
24. B
25. C

EXAMINATION SECTION

TEST 1

DIRECTIONS: Each question or incomplete statement is followed by several suggested answers or completions. Select the one that BEST answers the question or completes the statement. *PRINT THE LETTER OF THE CORRECT ANSWER IN THE SPACE AT THE RIGHT.*

1. Good procedure in handling complaints from the public may be divided into the following four principal stages: 1.____
   I. Investigation of the complaint
   II. Receipt of the complaint
   III. Assignment of responsibility for investigation and correction
   IV. Notification of correction

   The ORDER in which these stages ordinarily come is:
   A. III, II, I, IV B. II, III, I, IV C. II, III, IV, I D. II, IV, III, I

2. The department may expect the MOST severe public criticism if 2.____
   A. it asks for an increase in its annual budget
   B. it purchases new and costly street cleaning equipment
   C. sanitation officers and men are reclassified to higher salary grades
   D. there is delay in cleaning streets of snow

3. The MOST important function of public relations in the department should be to 3.____
   A. develop cooperation on the part of the public in keeping streets clean
   B. get stricter penalties enacted for health code violations
   C. recruit candidates for entrance positions who ca be developed into supervisors
   D. train career personnel so that they can advance in the department

4. The one of the following which has MOST frequently elicited unfavorable public comment has been 4.____
   A. dirty sidewalks or streets B. dumping on lot
   C. failure to curb dogs D. overflowing garbage cans

5. It has been suggested that, as a public relations measure, sections hold *open house* for the public. 5.____
   The MOST effective time for this would be
   A. during the summer when children are not in school and can accompany their parents
   B. during the winter when show is likely to fall and the public can see snow removal preparations
   C. immediately after a heavy snow storm when department snow removal operations are in full progress
   D. when street sanitation is receiving general attention as during *Keep City Clean* week

6. When a public agency conducts a public relations program, it is MOST likely to find that each recipient of its message will 6.____
   A. disagree with the basic purpose of the message if the officials are not well known to him
   B. accept the message if it is presented by someone perceived as having a definite intention to persuade
   C. ignore the message unless it is presented in a literate and clever manner
   D. give greater attention to certain portions of the message as a result of his individual and cultural differences

7. Following are three statements about public relations and communications: 7.____
   I. A person who seeks to influence public opinion can speed up a trend
   II. Mass communications is the exposure of a mass audience to an idea
   III. All media are equally effective in reaching opinion leaders
   Which of the following choices CORRECTLY classifies the above statements into those which are correct and those which are not?
   A. I and II are correct, but III is not.
   B. II and III are correct, but I is not.
   C. I and III are correct, but II is not.
   D III is correct, but I and II are not.

8. Public relations experts say that MAXIMUM effect for a message results from 8.____
   A. concentrating in one medium
   B. ignoring mass media and concentrating on *opinion makers*
   C. presenting only those factors which support a given position
   D. using a combination of two or more of the available media

9. To assure credibility and avoid hostility, the public relations man MUST 9.____
   A. make certain his message is truthful, not evasive or exaggerated
   B. make sure his message contains some dire consequence if ignored
   C. repeat the message often enough so that it cannot be ignored
   D. try to reach as many people and groups as possible

10. The public relations man MUST be prepared to assume that members of his audience 10.____
   A. may have developed attitudes toward his proposals—favorable, neutral, or unfavorable
   B. will be immediately hostile
   C. will consider his proposals with an open mind
   D. will invariably need an introduction to his subject

11. The one of the following statements that is CORRECT is: 11.____
   A. When a stupid question is asked of you by the public, it should be disregarded
   B. If you insist on formality between you and the public, the public will not be able to ask stupid questions that cannot be answered
   C. The public should be treated courteously, regardless of how stupid their questions may be
   D. You should explain to the public how stupid their questions are

12. With regard to public relations, the MOST important item which should be emphasized in an employee training program is that 12.____
    A. each inspector is a public relations agent
    B an inspector should give the public all the information it asks for
    C. it is better to make mistakes and give erroneous information than to tell the public that you do not know the correct answer to their problem
    D. public relations is so specialized a field that only persons specially trained in it should consider it

13. Members of the public frequently ask about departmental procedures. Of the following, it is BEST to 13.____
    A. advise the public to put the question in writing so that he can get a proper formal reply
    B. refuse to answer because this is a confidential matter
    C. explain the procedure as briefly as possible
    D. attempt to avoid the issue by discussing other matters

14. The effectiveness of a public relations program in a public agency such as the authority is BEST indicated by the 14.____
    A. amount of mass media publicity favorable to the policies of the authority
    B. morale of those employees who directly serve the patrons of the authority
    C. public's understanding and support of the authority's program and policies
    D. number of complaint received by the authority from patrons using its facilities

15. In an attempt to improve public opinion about a certain idea, the BEST course of action for an agency to take would be to present the 15.____
    A. clearest statements of the idea even though the language is somewhat technical
    B. idea as the result of long-term studies
    C. idea in association with something familiar to most people
    D. idea as the viewpoint of the majority leaders

16. The fundamental factor in any agency's community relations program is 16.____
    A. an outline of the objectives
    B. relations with the media
    C. the everyday actions of the employees
    D. a well-planned supervisory program

17. The FUNDAMENTAL factor in the success of a community relations program is 17.____
    A. true commitment by the community
    B. true commitment by the administration
    C. a well-planned, systematic approach
    D. the actions of individuals in their contacts with the public

18. The statement below which is LEAST correct is: 18.____
    A. Because of selection standards, the supervisor frequently encounters problems resulting from subordinates' inability to express themselves in the language of the profession.
    B. Distortion of the meaning of a communication is usually brought about by a failure to use language that has a precise meaning to others.
    C. The term *filtering* is the distortion or dilution of content of a communication that occurs as information is passed from individual to individual.
    D. The complexity of the *communications net* will directly affect.

19. Consider the following three statements that may or may not be CORRECT: 19.____
    I. In order to prevent the stifling of communications flow, supervisors should insist that employees use the formal communications network.
    II. Two-way communications are faster and more accurate than one-way communications.
    III. There is a direct correlation between the effectiveness of communications and the total setting in which they occur.

    The choice below which MOST accurately describes the above statement is:
    A. All three are correct.
    B. All three are incorrect.
    C. More than one statement is correct.
    D. Only one of the statements is correct.

20. The statement below which is MOST inaccurate is: 20.____
    A. The supervisor's most important tool in learning whether or not he is communicating well is feedback.
    B. Follow-up is essential if useful feedback is to be obtained.
    C. Subordinates are entitled, as a matter of right, to explanations from management concerning the reasons for orders or directives.
    D. A skilled supervisor is often able to use the grapevine to good advantage.

21. *Since concurrence by those affected is not sought, this kind of communication can be issued with relative ease.* 21.____

    The kind of communication being referred to in this quotation is
    A. autocratic B. democratic C. directive D. free-rein

22. The statement below which is LEAST correct is: 22.___
    A. Clarity is more important in oral communicating than in written since the readers of a written communication can read it over again.
    B. Excessive use of abbreviations in written communications should be avoided.
    C. Short sentences with simple words are preferred over complex sentences and difficult words in a written communication.
    D. The *newspaper* style of writing ordinarily simplifies expression and facilitates understanding.

23. Which one of the following is the MOST important factor for the department to consider in building a good public image? 23.____
   A. A good working relationship with the news media
   B. An efficient community relations program
   C. An efficient system for handling citizen complaints
   D. The proper maintenance of facilities and equipment
   E. The behavior of individuals in their contacts with the public.

24. It has been said that the ability to communicate clearly and concisely is the MOST important single skill of the supervisor. 24.____
Consider the following statements:
   I. The adage, *Actions speak louder than words*, has NO application in superior/subordinate communications since good communications are accomplished with words.
   II. The environment in which a communication takes place will *rarely* determine its effect.
   III. Words are symbolic representations which must be associated with past experience or else they are meaningless.
The choice below which MOST accurately describes the above statements is:
   A. I, II, and III are correct.
   B. I and II are correct, but III is not.
   C. I and III are correct, but II is not.
   D. III is correct, but I and II are not.
   E. I, II, and III are incorrect.

25. According to expert opinion, the effectiveness of an organization is very dependent upon good upward, downward, and lateral communications. Lateral communications are most important to the activity of coordinating the efforts of organizational units. Before real communication can take place at any level, barriers to communication must be recognized, understood, and removed. 25.____
Consider the following three statements:
   I. The *principal* barrier to good communications is a failure to establish empathy between sender and receiver.
   II. The difference in status or rank between the sender and receiver of a communication may be a communications barrier.
   III. Communications are easier if they travel upward from subordinate to superior
The choice below which MOST accurately describes the above statements is:
   A. I, II and III are incorrect.
   B. I and II are incorrect.
   C. I, II, and III are correct.
   D. I and II are correct.
   E. I and III are incorrect.

KEY (CORRECT ANSWERS)

1.	B	11.	C
2.	D	12.	A
3.	A	13.	C
4.	A	14.	C
5.	D	15.	C
6.	D	16.	C
7.	A	17.	D
8.	D	18.	A
9.	A	19.	D
10.	A	20.	C

21. A
22. A
23. E
24. D
25. E

PREPARING WRITTEN MATERIALS

EXAMINATION SECTION

TEST 1

DIRECTIONS: Each question consists of a sentence which may be classified appropriately under one of the following four categories:

A. Incorrect because of faulty grammar or sentence structure;
B. Incorrect because of faulty punctuation;
C. Incorrect because of faulty capitalization;
D. Correct

Examine each sentence carefully. Then, in the space at the right, indicate the letter preceding the category which is the BEST of the four suggested above. Each incorrect sentence contains only one type of error. Consider a sentence correct if it contains no errors, although there may be other correct ways of expressing the same thought.

1. All the employees, in this office, are over twenty-one years old. 1.____

2. Neither the clerk nor the stenographer was able to explain what had happened. 2.____

3. Mr. Johnson did not know who he would assign to type the order. 3.____

4. Mr. Marshall called her to report for work on Saturday. 4.____

5. He might of arrived on time if the train has not been delayed. 5.____

6. Some employees on the other hand, are required to fill out these forms every month. 6.____

7. The supervisor issued special instructions to his subordinates to prevent their making errors. 7.____

8. Our supervisor Mr. Williams, expects to be promoted in about two weeks. 8.____

9. We were informed that prof. Morgan would attend the conference. 9.____

10. The clerks were assigned to the old building; the stenographers, to the new building. 10.____

11. The supervisor asked Mr. Smith and I to complete the work as quickly as possible. 11.____

12. He said, that before an employee can be permitted to leave, the report must be finished. 12.____

13. A calculator, in addition to the three computers, are needed in the new office. 13.____

14. Having made many errs in her work, the supervisor asked the typist to be more careful. 14.____

15. "If you are given an assignment," he said, "you should begin work on it as quickly as possible." 15.____

16. All the clerks, including those who have been appointed recently are required to work on the new assignment. 16.____

17. The office manager asked each employee to work one Saturday a month. 17.____

18. Neither Mr. Smith nor Mr. Jones was able to finish his assignment on time. 18.____

19. The task of filing these cards is to be divided equally between you and he. 19.____

20. He is an employee whom we consider to be efficient. 20.____

21. I believe that the new employees are not as punctual as us. 21.____

22. The employees, working in this office, are to be congratulated for their work. 22.____

23. The delay in preparing the report was caused, in his opinion, by the lack of proper supervision and coordination. 23.____

24. John Jones accidentally pushed the wrong button and then all the lights went out. 24.____

25. The investigator ought to of had the witness sign the statement. 25.____

KEY (CORRECT ANSWERS)

1.	B	11.	A
2.	D	12.	B
3.	A	13.	A
4.	C	14.	A
5.	A	15.	D
6.	B	16.	B
7.	D	17.	C
8.	B	18.	D
9.	C	19.	A
10.	D	20.	D

21.	A
22.	B
23.	D
24.	D
25.	A

TEST 2

Questions 1-10.

DIRECTIONS: Each of the following sentences may be classified under one of the following four options:

A. Faulty; contains an error in grammar only
B. Faulty; contains an error in spelling only
C. Faulty; contains an error in grammar and an error in spelling
D. Correct; contains no error in grammar or in spelling

Examine each sentence carefully to determine under which of the above four options it is BEST classified. Then, in the space at the right, write the letter preceding the option which is the best of the four listed above.

1. A recognized principle of good management is that an assignment should be given to whomever is best qualified to carry it out. 1.____

2. He considered it a privilege to be allowed to review and summarize the technical reports issued annually by your agency. 2.____

3. Because the warehouse was in an inaccessible location, deliveries of electric fixtures from the warehouse were made only in large lots. 3.____

4. Having requisitioned the office supplies, Miss Brown returned to her desk and resumed the computation of petty cash disbursements. 4.____

5. One of the advantages of this chemical solution is that records treated with it are not inflamable. 5.____

6. The complaint of this employee, in addition to the complaints of the other employees, were submitted to the grievance committee. 6.____

7. A study of the duties and responsibilities of each of the various categories of employees was conducted by an unprejudiced classification analyst. 7.____

8. Ties of friendship with this subordinate compels him to withold the censure that the subordinate deserves. 8.____

9. Neither of the agencies are affected by the decision to institute a program for rehabilitating physically handi-caped men and women. 9.____

10. The chairman stated that the argument between you and he was creating an intolerable situation. 10.____

Questions 11-25.

DIRECTIONS: Each of the following sentences may be classified under one of the following four options:

A. Correct
B. Sentence contains an error in spelling
C. Sentence contains an error in grammar
D. Sentence contains errors in both grammar and spelling.

11. He reported that he had had a really good time during his vacation although the farm was located in a very inaccessible portion of the country. 11.____

12. It looks to me like he has been fasinated by that beautiful painting. 12.____

13. We have permitted these kind of pencils to accumulate on our shelves, knowing we can sell them at a profit of five cents apiece any time we choose. 13.____

14. Believing that you will want an unexagerated estimate of the amount of business we can expect, I have made every effort to secure accurate figures. 14.____

15. Each and every man, woman and child in that untrammeled wilderness carry guns for protection against the wild animals. 15.____

16. Although this process is different than the one to which he is accustomed, a good chemist will have no trouble. 16.____

17. Insensible to the fuming and fretting going on about him, the engineer continued to drive the mammoth dynamo to its utmost capacity. 17.____

18. Everyone had studied his lesson carefully and was consequently well prepared when the instructor began to discuss the fourth dimention. 18.____

19. I learned Johnny six new arithmetic problems this afternoon. 19.____

20. Athletics is urged by our most prominent citizens as the pursuit which will enable the younger generation to achieve that ideal of education, a sound mind in a sound body. 20.____

21. He did not see whoever was at the door very clearly but thinks it was the city tax appraiser. 21.____

22. He could not scarsely believe that his theories had been substantiated in this convincing fashion. 22.____

23. Although you have displayed great ingenuity in carrying out your assignments, the choice for the position still lies among Brown and Smith. 23.____

24. If they had have pleaded at the time that Smith was an accessory to the crime, it would have lessened the punishment. 24.____

25. It has proven indispensible in his compilation of the facts in the matter. 25.____

KEY (CORRECT ANSWERS)

1. A
2. D
3. B
4. D
5. B

6. A
7. D
8. C
9. C
10. A

11. A
12. D
13. C
14. B
15. D

16. C
17. A
18. B
19. C
20. A

21. B
22. D
23. C
24. D
25. B

TEST 3

Questions 1-5.

DIRECTIONS: Questions 1 through 5 consist of sentences which may or may not contain errors in grammar or spelling or both. Sentences which do not contain errors in grammar or spelling or both are to be considered correct, even though there may be other correct ways of expressing the same thought. Examine each sentence carefully. Then, in the space at the right, write the letter of the answer which is the BEST of those suggested below.

A. If the sentence is correct
B. If the sentence contains an error in spelling
C. If the sentence contains an error in grammar
D. If the sentence contains errors in both grammar and spelling.

1. Brown is doing fine although the work is irrevelant to his training. 1.____

2. The conference of sales managers voted to set its adjournment at one o'clock in order to give those present an opportunity to get rid of all merchandise. 2.____

3. He decided that in view of what had taken place at the hotel that he ought to stay and thank the benificent stranger who had rescued him from an embarassing situation. 3.____

4. Since you object to me criticizing your letter, I have no alternative but to consider you a mercenary scoundrel. 4.____

5. I rushed home ahead of schedule so that you will leave me go to the picnic with Mary. 5.____

Questions 6-15.

DIRECTIONS: Some of the following sentences contain an error in spelling, word usage, or sentence structure, or punctuation. Some sentences are correct as they stand although there may be other correct ways of expressing the same thought. All incorrect sentences contain only one error. Mark your answer to each question in the space at the right as follows:

A. If the sentence has an error in spelling
B. If the sentence has an error in punctuation or capitalization
C. If the sentence has an error in word usage or sentence structure
D. If the sentence is correct

6. Because the chairman failed to keep the participants from wandering off into irrelevant discussions, it was impossible to reach a consensus before the meeting was adjourned. 6.____

7. Certain employers have an unwritten rule that any applicant, who is over 55 years of age, is automatically excluded from consideration for any position whatsoever. 7.____

8. If the proposal to build schools in some new apartment buildings were to be accepted by the builders, one of the advantages that could be expected to result would be better communication between teachers and parents of schoolchildren. 8.____

9. In this instance, the manufacturer's violation of the law against deseptive packaging was discernible only to an experienced inspector. 9.____

10. The tenants' anger stemmed from the president's going to Washington to testify without consulting them first. 10.____

11. Did the president of this eminent banking company say; "We intend to hire and train a number of these disadvantaged youths?" 11.____

12. In addition, today's confidential secretary must be knowledgable in many different areas: for example, she must know modern techniques for making travel arrangements for the executive. 12.____

13. To avoid further disruption of work in the offices, the protesters were forbidden from entering the building unless they had special passes. 13.____

14. A valuable secondary result of our training conferences is the opportunities afforded for management to observe the reactions of the participants. 14.____

15. Of the two proposals submitted by the committee, the first one is the best. 15.____

Questions 16-25.

DIRECTIONS: Each of the following sentences may be classified MOST appropriately under one of the following three categories:

A. Faulty because of incorrect grammar
B. Faulty because of incorrect punctuation
C. Correct

Examine each sentence. Then, print the capital letter preceding the BEST choice of the three suggested above. All incorrect sentences contain only one type of error. Consider a sentence correct if it contains none of the types of errors mentioned, even though there may be other ways of expressing the same thought.

16. He sent the notice to the clerk who you hired yesterday. 16.____

17. It must be admitted, however that you were not informed of this change. 17.____

18. Only the employees who have served in this grade for at least two years are eligible for promotion. 18.____

19. The work was divided equally between she and Mary. 19.____

20. He thought that you were not available at that time. 20.____

21. When the messenger returns; please give him this package. 21.____

22. The new secretary prepared, typed, addressed, and delivered, the notices. 22.____

23. Walking into the room, his desk can be seen at the rear. 23.____

24. Although John has worked here longer than she, he produces a smaller amount of work. 24.____

25. She said she could of typed this report yesterday. 25.____

KEY (CORRECT ANSWERS)

1. D
2. A
3. D
4. C
5. C

6. A
7. B
8. D
9. A
10. D

11. B
12. A
13. C
14. D
15. C

16. A
17. B
18. C
19. A
20. C

21. B
22. B
23. A
24. C
25. A

TEST 4

Questions 1-5.

DIRECTIONS: Each of the following sentences may be classified MOST appropriately under one of the following three categories:

A. Faulty because of incorrect grammar
B. Faulty because of incorrect punctuation
C. Correct

Examine each sentence. Then, print the capital letter preceding the BEST choice of the three suggested above. All incorrect sentences contain only one type of error. Consider a sentence correct if it contains none of the types of errors mentioned, even though there may be other ways of expressing the same thought.

1. Neither one of these procedures are adequate for the efficient performance of this task. 1.____

2. The keyboard is the tool of the typist; the cash register, the tool of the cashier. 2.____

3. "The assignment must be completed as soon as possible" said the supervisor. 3.____

4. As you know, office handbooks are issued to all new employees. 4.____

5. Writing a speech is sometimes easier than to deliver it before an audience. 5.____

Questions 6-15.

DIRECTIONS: Each statement given in Questions 6 through 15 contains one of the faults of English usage listed below. For each, choose from the options listed the MAJOR fault contained.

A. The statement is not a complete sentence.
B. The statement contains a word or phrase that is redundant.
C. The statement contains a long, less commonly used word when a shorter, more direct word would be acceptable.
D. The statement contains a colloquial expression that normally is avoided in business writing.

6. The fact that this activity will afford an opportunity to meet your group. 6.____

7. Do you think that the two groups can join together for next month's meeting? 7.____

8. This is one of the most exciting new innovations to be introduced into our college. 8.____

9. We expect to consummate the agenda before the meeting ends tomorrow at noon. 9.____

10. While this seminar room is small in size, we think we can use it. 10.____

11. Do you think you can make a modification in the date of the Budget Committee meeting? 11.____

12. We are cognizant of the problem but we think we can ameliorate the situation. 12.____

13. Shall I call you around three on the day I arrive in the City? 13.____

14. Until such time that we know precisely that the students will be present. 14.____

15. The consensus of opinion of all the members present is reported in the minutes. 15.____

Questions 16-25.

DIRECTIONS: For each of Questions 16 through 25, select from the options given below the MOST applicable choice.

A. The sentence is correct.
B. The sentence contains a spelling error only.
C. The sentence contains an English grammar error only.
D. The sentence contains both a spelling error and an English grammar error.

16. Every person in the group is going to do his share. 16.____

17. The man who we selected is new to this University. 17.____

18. She is the older of the four secretaries on the two staffs that are to be combined. 18.____

19. The decision has to be made between him and I. 19.____

20. One of the volunteers are too young for his complicated task, don't you think? 20.____

21. I think your idea is splindid and it will improve this report considerably. 21.____

22. Do you think this is an exagerated account of the behavior you and me observed this morning? 22.____

23. Our supervisor has a clear idea of excelence. 23.____

24. How many occurences were verified by the observers? 24.____

25. We must complete the typing of the draft of the questionaire by noon tomorrow. 25.____

KEY (CORRECT ANSWERS)

1.	A	11.	C
2.	C	12.	C
3.	B	13.	D
4.	C	14.	A
5.	A	15.	B
6.	A	16.	A
7.	B	17.	C
8.	B	18.	C
9.	C	19.	C
10.	B	20.	D

21.	B
22.	D
23.	B
24.	B
25.	B

PREPARING WRITTEN MATERIAL

EXAMINATION SECTION

TEST 1

DIRECTIONS: Each of the following sentences may be classified under one of the following four categories:
A. *Faulty* because of incorrect grammar or usage
B. *Faulty* because of incorrect punctuation or spelling
C. *Faulty* because of incorrect capitalization
D. *Correct*

Examine each sentence carefully. Then, in the correspondingly numbered space on the right, print the capital letter preceding the option which is the best of the four suggested above.

(All incorrect sentences contain but one type of error. Consider a sentence correct if it contains none of the types of errors mentioned, even though there may be other correct ways of expressing the same thought.

1. They gave the poor man some food when he approached. 1.____

2. I regret the loss caused by the error. 2.____

3. The students have a new teacher for shop mantenance. 3.____

4. They sweared to bring out all the facts. 4.____

5. He decided to open a branch store on 33rd street. 5.____

6. His speed is equal and more than that of a racehorse. 6.____

7. He felt very warm on that Summer day. 7.____

8. He was assisted by his friend, who lives in the next house. 8.____

9. The climate of New York is colder than California. 9.____

10. I shall wait for you on the corner. 10.____

11. Did we see the boy whose the leader? 11.____

12. Being a modest person, John seldom takes about his invention. 12.____

13. The gang is called the smith street boys. 13.____

14. He seen the man break into the store. 14.____

15. We expected to lay still there for quite a while. 15.____

16. He is considered to be the Leader of his organization. 16.____

17. Although He received an invitation, He won't go. 17.____

18. The letter must be here some place. 18.____

19. I thought it to be he. 19.____

20. We expect to remain here for a long time. 20.____

21. The committee was agreed. 21.____

22. Two-thirds of the building are finished. 22.____

23. The water was froze. 23.____

24. Everyone of the salesmen must supply their own car. 24.____

25. Who is the author of Gone With the Wind? 25.____

26. He marched on and declaring that he would never surrender. 26.____

27. Who shall I say called? 27.____

28. Everyone has left but they. 28.____

29. Who did we give the order to? 29.____

30. Send your order in immediately. 30.____

31. I believe I paid the Bill. 31.____

32. I have not met but one person. 32.____

33. Why aren't Tom, and Fred, going to the dance? 33.____

34. What reason is there for him not going? 34.____

35. The seige of Malta was a tremendous event. 35.____

36. I was there yesterday I assure you. 36.____

37. Your ukulele is better than mine. 37.____

38. No one was there only Mary. 38.____

39. The Capital city of Vermont is Montpelier. 39.____

40. Reggie Jackson may hit the largest amount of home runs this season. 40.____

KEY (CORRECT ANSWERS)

1.	B	11.	B	21.	D	31.	C
2.	D	12.	D	22.	A	32.	A
3.	B	13.	C	23.	A	33.	B
4.	A	14.	A	24.	A	34.	A
5.	C	15.	A	25.	B	35.	B
6.	A	16.	C	26.	A	36.	B
7.	C	17.	C	27.	D	37.	B
8.	D	18.	A	28.	D	38.	A
9.	A	19.	A	29.	A	39.	C
10.	D	20.	D	30.	D	40.	A

TEST 2

Questions 1-3.

DIRECTIONS: Questions 1 through 3 each consist of four sentences. Choose the one sentence in each set of four that would be BEST for a formal letter or report. Consider grammar and appropriate usage.

1. A. Most all the work he completed before he become ill. 1.____
   B. He completed most of the work before becoming ill.
   C. Prior to him becoming ill his work was mostly completed.
   D. Before he became will most of the work he had completed.

2. A. Being that the report lacked a clearly worded recommendation, it did not matter that it contained enough information. 2.____
   B. There was enough information in the report, although it, including the recommendation, were not clearly worded.
   C. Although the report contained enough information, it did not have a clearly worded recommendation.
   D. Though the report did not have a recommendation that was clearly worded, and the information therein contained was enough.

3. A. Having already overlooked the important mistakes, the ones which she found were not as important toward the end of the letter. 3.____
   B. Toward the end of the letter she had already overlooked the important mistakes, so that which she had found were not important.
   C. The mistakes which she had already overlooked were not as important as those which near the end of letter she had found.
   D. The mistakes which she found near the end of the letter were not so important as those which she had already overlooked.

Questions 4-5.

DIRECTIONS: Select the correct answer.

4. The unit has exceeded _____ goals and the employees are satisfied with _____ accomplishments. 4.____
   A. their; it's B. it's, it's C. is, there D. its, their

5. Research indicates that employees who _____ no opportunity for close social relationships often find their work unsatisfying, and this _____ of satisfaction often reflects itself in low production. 5.____
   A. have, lack B. have, excess C. has, lack D. has, excess

KEY (CORRECT ANSWERS)

1. B
2. C
3. D
4. D
5. A

TEST 3

DIRECTIONS: Select the choice which BEST expresses the thought and which contains NO errors in grammar or sentence construction.

1. A. She, hearing a signal, the source lamp flashed. 1.____
   B. While hearing a signal, the source lamp flashed
   C. In hearing a signal, the source lamp flashed.
   D. As she heard a signal, the source lamp flashed.

2. A. Every one of the time records have been initialed in the designated spaces. 2.____
   B. All of the time records has been initialed in the designated spaces.
   C. Which one of the time records was initialed in the designated spaces.
   D. The time records all been initialed in the designated spaces.

3. A. If there is no one else to answer the phone, you will have to answer it. 3.____
   B. You will have to answer it yourself if no one else answers the phone.
   C. If no one else is not around to pick up the phone, you have to do it.
   D. You will have to answer the phone when nobodys here to do it.

4. A. Dr. Byrnes not in his office. What could I do for you? 4.____
   B. Dr. Byrnes is not in his office. Is there something I can do for you?
   C. Since Dr. Byrnes is not in his office, might there be something I may do for you?
   D. Is there any ways I can assist you since Dr. Brynes is not in his office?

5. A. She do not understand how the new console works. 5.____
   B. The way the new console works, she doesn't understand.
   C. She doesn't understand how the new console works.
   D. The new console works, so that she doesn't understand.

KEY (CORRECT ANSWERS)

1. D
2. C
3. A
4. B
5. C

TEST 4

DIRECTIONS: The following questions each consist of a sentence which may or may not be an example of good English usage.

Consider grammar, punctuation, spelling, capitalization, awkwardness, etc.

Examine each sentence and then choose the correct statement about it from the four choices below. If the English usage in the sentence given is better than any of the changes suggested in options B, C, or D, choose option A. (Do not choose an option that will change the meaning of the sentence.)

1. The typist used an extention cord in order to connect her typewriter to the outlet nearest to her desk. 1.____
   A. This is an example of acceptable writing.
   B. A period should be placed after the word "cord" and the word "in" should have a capital "I."
   C. A comma should be placed after the word "typewriter."
   D. The word "extention" should be spelled "extension."

2. He would have went to the conference if he had received an invitation. 2.____
   A. This is an example of acceptable writing.
   B. The word "went" should be replaced by the word "gone."
   C. The word "had" should be replaced by "would have."
   D. The word "conference" should be spelled "conference."

3. In order to make the report neater, he spent many hours rewriting it. 3.____
   A. This is an example of acceptable writing.
   B. The word "more" should be inserted before the word "neater."
   C. There should be a colon after the word "neater."
   D. The word "spent" should be changed to "have spent."

4. His supervisor told him that he should of read the memorandum more carefully. 4.____
   A. This is an example of acceptable writing.
   B. The word "memorandum" should be spelled "memorandom."
   C. The word "of" should be replaced by the word "have."
   D. The word "carefully" should be replaced by the word "have."

5. It was decided that two separate reports should be written. 5.____
   A. This is an example of acceptable writing.
   B. A comma should be inserted after the word "decided."
   C. The word "be" should be replaced by the word "been."
   D. A colon should be inserted after the word "that."

6. She don't seem to understand that the work must be done as soon as possible. 6.____
   A. This is an example of acceptable writing.
   B. The word "doesn't" should replace the word "don't."
   C. The word "why" should replace the word "that."
   D. The word "as" before the word "soon" should be eliminated.

KEY (CORRECT ANSWERS)

1. D
2. B
3. A
4. C
5. A
6. B

GUIDELINES FOR EFFECTIVE TELEPHONE COMMUNICATIONS

"Telephone" come from a Greek word, which means "to speak at a distance."

Business and non-business calls combined, billions of telephone calls are completed on an average day throughout the year.

Telephone selling is more personal and more direct than selling through the mail.

The telephone may be used in telephone marketing for 1) order solicitation, 2) to set up sales appointments, 3) lead generation, 4) renewals (calls to present customers for repeat business), 5) marginal account coverage (to contact client accounts whose volume is too small.

The following suggestions are offered to the general public, telephone operators, office personnel salesmen, and executives.

1. BE FRIENDLY—Some busy executives release their daily tensions on the telephone. They become impatient, irritated and even hostile.
   The effective communicator maintains a positive mental attitude when speaking on the phone.
2. IMPROVE YOUR VOICE RANGE—A lowered voice sounds warmer and friendlier than a high pitched voice. If you tend to use a high pitched voice, you can take a pen or pencil in your hand and practice lowering your voice as you lower the object in your hand. Repeating this exercise while speaking on the phone will improve your speaking voice range.
3. GESTURE WHILE YOU SPEAK—Gestures are a part of human behavior that even computerized robots cannot duplicate. Gestures are a natural part of speaking behavior.
   Using gestures while you speak on the telephone will make your telephone voice more natural.
   Smile into the telephone-express yourself, show enthusiasm, get excited, and be sincere.
4. SAY WHAT YOU MEAN—People can't see your expression when you talk on the phone, so say what you want to express.
5. LISTEN CAREFULLY—If you do not listen carefully to what the other person is saying, you can't be sure that you're carrying on effective communication. Listen carefully so that the person you are speaking with does not say..."I know you believe you understand what you think I said. But I'm not sure you realize that what you heard is not what I meant."
6. BE COURTEOUS—You are more likely to get cooperation if you make your requests politely.
7. SIMPLIFY YOUR MESSAGE—Make separate calls for different purposes. If you have to make separate points, state them clearly by using numerical identification. For example, point one, point two and point three.
8. STRUCTURE YOUR CONVERSATION—Think about the purpose of different types of calls and how you can structure them so that you can communicate most effectively. The more effectively you communicate on the phone, the more time you save.
9. EXPRESS YOURSELF CLEARLY—In seeking to give style and effectiveness to the wording and phrasing of a speech, one must never forget that clearness of expression is the first imperative. Everything in style must yield to clarity.

10. PACE YOUR CONVERSATION – Don't speak too slowly, otherwise you will bore your listener.
People are more attentive when you speak at a quick pace, provided that you are not speaking so fast that others cannot understand what you are saying.

www.ingramcontent.com/pod-product-compliance
Lightning Source LLC
Chambersburg PA
CBHW082211300426
44117CB00016B/2762